INFORMAL WELFARE

Informal Welfare

A Sociological Study of Care in Northern Ireland

ROSANNE CECIL,
JOHN OFFER
and
FRED ST. LEGER,

*Department of Social Administration and Policy,
University of Ulster at Coleraine*

Gower

Published by
Gower Publishing Company Limited
Gower House
Croft Road
Aldershot
Hants GU11 3HR
England

Published by
Gower Publishing Company
Old Post Road
Brookfield
Vermont 05036
USA

British Library Cataloguing in Publication Data

Cecil, R.
  Informal welfare : a sociological study
  of care in Northern Ireland.
  1. Volunteer workers in social service——
  Northern Ireland 2. Social service, Rural
  ——Northern Ireland
  I. Title II. Offer, J. III. St. Leger,F.
  361.3'7'09416   HV249.N68

  ISBN 0-566-05099-4

Printed and bound in Great Britain by
Paradigm Print, Bungay, Suffolk

Contents

Preface

Our research into informal welfare was triggered by two separate developments. On the one hand, discussions about social policy were becoming increasingly interested in how informal care could in some way be 'tapped' by social workers. On the other hand, sociologists working in the field of welfare were finding that, for their own reasons, research into informal welfare was a high priority. What we have tried to achieve is a book which contributes both to the development of the sociology of welfare and to the evaluation and making of policy. In the context of a rural community in Northern Ireland, we studied, in particular the distribution of informal welfare in relation to specific types of need; the main features of informal welfare, including the attitudes, perceptions and motivations both of the givers and receivers of help; and the relationship of informal welfare to voluntary and statutory sources of help. We have also commented on the delivery of social work services in relation to informal welfare, paying special regard to the need to avoid damaging it; on training; and on the directions which should be taken by future cognate research.

Chapter 1 introduces informal welfare as a topic needing to be studied, and the manner in which this should be done. (Sections of this chapter are revisions of parts of contributions by one of us to the Year Book of Social Policy in Britain 1984-5 edited by M. Brenton and C. Jones and published by Routledge and Kegan Paul, and to the British Journal of Social Work vol. 14, no. 6, 1984). For reasons we discuss we felt that it was very important to start the research by looking at caring activities through the eyes of those involved. Hence a largely ethnographic approach was adopted. A relatively small rural community was chosen for the research - Glengow we call it, and it and the methods we used are described in the next chapter. Following an overview of the family, chapters 4, 5 and 6 discuss care given within the family and by neighbours, and the problems (and satisfactions) of being an informal carer. The next four chapters look at the care received by disabled children, the disabled elderly, and the relatively 'fit' elderly. Chapter 11 summarises our main findings and also presents some related comments on policy matters and future research.

In several chapters we include as quotations the words of our respondents. On a few occasions they have been lightly edited in order to make their meaning as clear as possible.

We believe we have both complemented and supplemented the results of other studies of informal welfare. In doing so we have incurred many debts. The DHSS (NI) made the study of Glengow possible by funding us over a two-year period (Michael Pyper there was of particular help to us). Professor Peter Stringer of the Policy Research Institute in Northern Ireland gave us invaluable financial assistance during the difficult period when book emerged from Report. Valerie Canny, Carol Kealey, Karen McCulloch, Irene Simpson and Donna Hargie have given us extensive and valued support as typists. Staff in the University Library at Coleraine (particularly Pam Compton) and elsewhere in the University (particularly Norma Reid, Kate Thompson and Colin Todd) have been unfailingly helpful. PPRU carried out a survey for us with impressive efficiency. Last, but certainly not least, is the debt we owe to the people of Glengow. They tolerated hours of interviews, and we thank them sincerely. We made a subject for science people who showed us great kindness.

Whilst each chapter is the shared outcome of all three authors' work, primary contributions to chapters 2 to 7 were from Rosanne Cecil, to chapters 1 and 11, from John Offer, and chapters 8, 9 and 10 from Fred St Leger.

1 Informal welfare: background to the topic

In recent years informal welfare has been moving up the agenda both in
social policy itself and in the research activities of sociology and
social administration, particularly in the United Kingdom and the United
States. Indeed, social workers in the United Kingdom were urged by the
Barclay Report (1982) to adopt flexible organisational styles which take
informal welfare more into account. To a limited extent this was
already happening with the performance being eagerly monitored (for
example, Hadley and McGrath, 1984). There are at least five reasons
which account for such developments at the level of policy: political
parties, sometimes governments, have been seeking afresh to express
principles which define the 'proper' scope of state action; doubts have
been raised about the effectiveness of public spending in some areas of
provision, and about the nature of the impact of the bureaucracy
involved in much statutory provision on the users of those services, and
on relationships with voluntary agencies (see, for example, Hadley and
Hatch, 1981; and Knapp, 1984); a desire by governments in unkind
economic times simply to cut public expenditure budgets for welfare; a
focus within policy discussions on the notion of 'community care' [1];
a growth in groups within communities on the one hand calling for more
participation in the provision of statutory services and on the other
attempting to support informal carers, through giving advice and
practical help; and a growing amount of research on the subject,
especially so far as some specific 'problem' groups are concerned (see,
for example, Bayley, 1973; Wenger, 1984; and Parker, 1985). The
expansion of research itself probably owed much to the other factors.

---

[1] Parker has indicated a connection here (1985, p.4): 'As public
expenditure constraints have, increasingly, prompted the promotion
of "community care" as a policy goal, so the emphasis on measures
to implement that policy has shifted from statutory to informal and
voluntary provision'.

However, three additional and 'academic' reasons have been important in the justification of such research. Informal welfare was relatively uncharted and yet an apparently major 'division' of welfare; a natural subject for study, therefore. At the same time as this was recognised, roughly the early 1970s, two other reasons surfaced. The little research which had been undertaken on clients and potential clients was being criticised on the ground that the expectations held by them of formal welfare agencies needed to be understood in those clients' and potential clients' own terms, not in some way assumed. The study of informal welfare came to be seen as a way of improving the quality of such research, for informal welfare, as experienced by the participants, clearly affected any decision whether or not to contact formal agencies, and whether or not what was received was found satisfactory (see Mayer and Timms, 1970). A more abstract but not unrelated reason was that sociologists were coming to see that concepts in many areas of social life were given a plurality of meanings by the people involved which it was senseless to try to ignore or circumvent. It was necessary, therefore, to grasp the possibility at least of differences between 'professional' and 'everyday' definitions of situations, and, indeed, of differences within each grouping. Thus in order to understand the welfare field in general, let alone such topics as how people came to use social work services, or 'troubles' between clients and social workers, the study of the logic as well as the practice of informal welfare came to be viewed as an urgent matter (see Pinker, 1971, chs. 3, 4 and 5).

Nevertheless, the research output has been patchy in its coverage and, indeed, the sound point about a plurality of meanings has by no means always been absorbed. The three reasons, then, still hold true. They are the main reasons why this study was undertaken, and they explain the choice of methods and presentation. However, as we hope we show, the results permit what we believe are securely grounded comments on a range of ideas which have been expressed about the future of informal welfare and its relationships with formal agencies.

The remainder of this chapter seeks to set informal welfare and policies bearing upon it in some historical perspective; to define informal welfare with some precision; to consider contemporary policies towards it in the United Kingdom; and to review the current state of knowledge. At the end we caution that, our own study notwithstanding, not enough is yet known to suggest with safety major policy changes.

INFORMAL WELFARE IN HISTORICAL PERSPECTIVE

Informal welfare itself is not something new, and discussion of it has a long history. In their Report of 1834 the Poor Law Commissioners frequently indicated their conviction that an alleged dereliction of previously fulfilled familial responsibilities would be reversed by their proposals. Thus they claimed that the abolition of out-door relief to the able-bodied would, as well as repressing the fraudulent, 'obtain for others assistance from their friends, who are willing to see their relations pensioners, but would exert themselves to prevent their being inmates of a workhouse' (1974, p.392). Indeed, the wish to foster ever-better informal welfare networks was as a rule evident in the administration of the Poor Law, as well as in commentary on it and related matters. Thus T.S. Mackay, a leading light in both the Charity

Organisation Society and the Liberty and Property Defence League, as well as a prolific writer on the Poor Law, argued as follows in opposition to 'special proposals' to provide old age pensions (1891, p.296):

> it would be the height of presumption for the rough hand of the law to interfere to coerce or cajole the workman into preferring the remote risk of his own old age, which he may never live to see, to the more obvious claims of sickness, wife and children, more especially as a patient frugal attention to these will not leave his old age unprovided for.

Informal welfare also long ago attracted attention at a more explicitly sociological level. The evolutionist, Herbert Spencer, discussed it at length in his Social Statics (1851) and in the second volume of his Principles of Ethics (1893). Spencer carefully distinguished three kinds of welfare activity, thus highlighting an important social division of welfare (1893, p.376; see also Offer, 1983):

> We have the law-established relief for the poor by distribution of money compulsorily exacted; with which may fitly be joined the alms derived from endowments. We have relief of the poor carried on by spontaneously organized societies, to which funds are voluntarily contributed. And then, lastly, we have the help privately given – now to those who stand in some relation of dependence, now to those concerning whose claims partial knowledge has been obtained, and now hap-hazard to beggars.

Having thus distinguished between 'statutory', 'voluntary' and 'informal welfare', Spencer went on to suggest that each individual is surrounded by a 'special plexus' of social relations, the members of which have claims on each other in times of trouble. Although Spencer ended his discussion with some 'theoretical' reservations he could write as follows (1893, p. 391):

> Already all householders moderately endowed with sympathy, feel bound to care for their servants during illness; already they help those living out of the house who in less direct ways labour for them; already from time to time small traders, porters, errand boys, and the like, benefit by their kind offices on occasions of misfortune. The sole requisite seems to be that the usage which thus shows itself here and there irregularly should be called into general activity by the gradual disappearance of artificial agencies for distributing aid.

But by the time Spencer's words appeared the current of opinion was already flowing otherwise. The facts about poverty produced by Booth and later Rowntree indicated that, by certain specified standards, informal help was woefully inadequate. Political philosophies more sympathetic to strong action by governments over 'social' matters – such as that propounded by T.H. Green – were also making their mark. Burdens were to be lifted from families, relegating informal helping to altogether less essential work. Of course the full fruits of such a 'new way of ideas' did not appear until the late 1940s. However, long before then – as well as for many years after – neither governmental nor academic interest in informal welfare was very conspicuous. Social services provided by the state, staffed by experts on 'needs', received all the attention (see, for example, the Seebohm Report – <u>Report of the Committee on Local Authority and Allied Personal Social Services, 1968</u> – the document which established the structure of social work services as they are today in the United Kingdom, and the 'generic' nature of social work training and most practice). Indeed, one might reasonably suspect that writers such as the Webbs felt deep down that informal welfare ought even to be <u>discouraged</u>, because of its lack of 'expertise'.

It is, then, understandable if not excusable that only recently has social policy itself, together with academic writing on welfare matters, begun again seriously to acknowledge informal welfare. One would, for example, look in vain to the books of Titmuss for any discussion of it, in spite of his own work on the 'social division of welfare' [1]. Indeed, it is even now frequently ignored. There is no mention of it, for instance, in a textbook as popular as Hill's <u>Understanding Social Policy</u> (1980).

WHAT EXACTLY IS 'INFORMAL WELFARE'?

It is important to stress that 'informal welfare' should not be confused either with the help provided by voluntary organisations, or (following Gottlieb, 1981, p.30) with that provided by mutual-help groups. This is emphatically not to disagree with the Wolfenden Report's observation that (1978, p.28):

> Certain kinds of voluntary organisations could be expected to grow out of the informal system when it became apparent that informal methods were no longer adequate to meet the needs concerned. For example, informal arrangements for pre-school children might lead to the formation of a play group...

But it is to depart from Pinker when he comments (1979, p.46):

> 'Formal' practices of social welfare are the institutional activities which are entirely or largely governed by statute ... 'Informal' practices are the aspects of social welfare which are entirely or largely the spontaneous activities of ordinary citizens, either in groups or as individuals. The distinction is a useful one, provided that it is loosely drawn and treated as provisional, because the scope of voluntary effort and mutual aid is sometimes influenced by statute...

It seems more satisfactory clearly to locate voluntary organisations within the 'formal' category. The crucial principle for deciding the category to which they and other welfare activities belong is the obvious one: 'organised' arrangements must be 'formal'. Whether or not the scope of voluntary organisations is influenced by statute is a secondary matter.

---

[1] See especially R.M. Titmuss, 1958, ch. 2.

'Informal welfare' here comprises the help given to individuals by nuclear and extended families, and by neighbours and friends. It is taken to involve financial help as well as non-financial material help, along with physical care, emotional support and guidance. The Wolfenden Report observes that informal welfare is probably substantial in quantity: 'we have no doubt that a great deal more of it goes on than is commonly recognised' (1978, p.12). The Barclay Report adopts a similar line (1982, p.200):

> It is difficult to over-estimate the importance of the social care that members of communities give each other. The majority of people in trouble turn first to their own families for support. If this is lacking or insufficient, the help of wider kin, friends or neighbours becomes a valued resource – first because people we know are often (though by no means always) easier to talk to and confide in than workers in public agencies, secondly because seeking help from our informal networks is, within limits, socially acceptable.

However, as will be discussed below, such observations – though plausible – remain in need of further research to be adequately supported.

Two further points need to be made now, but which will be developed subsequently. First, help given informally may be a consequence of larger ambitions than a desire to help per se. For example, there may be a desire to shape the appropriate neighbourhood in a particular way (such as 'keeping it tidy'). This suggests that, to understand the dynamics of informal help, the contexts in which it is given – or not given – need to be carefully explored. Second, and not entirely unrelated, what counts in informal help as 'a good outcome' or as 'promoting welfare' might not be the same as 'welfare professionals' would so judge. Thus, as Froland et al. point out (1981, p.260):

> In everyday practice, professionals and informal caregivers have to grapple with different assumptions and expectations about what 'support' means and how it should be provided ... In many ways, trying to combine the efforts of professional service providers with those of family members, concerned neighbours, and devoted friends, is like trying to link two cultures in which very different beliefs, customs and norms of exchange prevail.

PRESENT SOCIAL POLICY AND INFORMAL WELFARE

By any standards the Wolfenden Report and the Barclay Report are important policy documents. They are already having some impact on the delivery of the relevant services in the United Kingdom. Both Reports went out of their way seriously to consider informal welfare in their recommendations and in the present section we review what they had to say in this connection.

On informal welfare, the tone of The Future of Voluntary Organisations is in general more cautious than is that of the Barclay Report. Wolfenden argues that, in relation to informal welfare, voluntary organisations can have three roles: they can replace it (where it has broken down, for example); they can temporarily relieve it; and they can reinforce it – helping it to flourish by, for example, passing on knowledge. This third role is the one the Wolfenden Committee wish to see expanded most. The Report did not – rightly we think – suggest that informal welfare will atrophy if such help is not forthcoming. In a changing society, one with improving communications and mobility and people living longer, they see informal welfare as changing, but not declining. Understandably, however, it cautions gently against either the state or the voluntary sector attempting to 'offload' existing responsibilities on to informal welfare networks. Informal welfare may be a 'main line of defence against many kinds of adversity' (1978, p.21), but it must be remembered that it varies in strength from time to time and place to place, and that it often lacks the financial resources or knowledge to provide the sort of care and support in such contexts as acute illness or unemployment which people in fact want, let alone ought to have (ibid., p.23). So, in addition to the recommendations noted above, the Report makes the following sensible call, after having noted the 'largely haphazard manner' in which formal help was related to informal help (ibid.):

> There would seem to be a good case for both statutory and voluntary organisations to undertake more systematic evaluations of these inter-relationships and to develop policies which more consistently and deliberately support the informal system.

However, the reply of the Labour Government (The Government and the Voluntary Sector, 1978) virtually ignored Wolfenden's comments on informal help. This lack of immediate interest in informal welfare in official circles, in spite of the Report's enthusiasm for it, was to some extent in contrast to the academic response. Nevertheless, opportunities were missed to develop matters. Hatch's (1980) mildly critical assessment of the Report – like the Report itself – failed to probe the assumption that the definitions of welfare embodied in informal welfare activities do not clash with those of formal agencies. Nor was much made of the perhaps too-cosy connotations of the Report's frequent mention of the informal system (see Offer, 1979).

The interest in informal welfare which had already been aroused in 'academic' circles began to expand in the late 1970s. However, and although Parker (1978) drew attention to some relevant questions posed in one DHSS discussion paper (A Happier Old Age, 1978), for a specific reflection of 'official' interest in informal welfare (as opposed to the broad and usually formal-orientated notion of 'community care') one has to look to the Barclay Report on social work.

The main Report urges social work to take more account of informal welfare. That clients themselves may be resources has, it argues, been too often overlooked (1982, p.111):

> If every client, family and social problem is seen as a need requiring formal social work help or intervention, social workers will always be expected and expecting to do too much. If, however, social workers see and draw out the potential in others, their ability, in conjunction with others, to respond to need will be enlarged.

The Report includes as skills needed in social work those which facilitate (ibid., p.151):

6

supporting volunteers or members of the family, or of a community, in direct contact with clients, and putting clients in touch with helping networks in local communities, acting indeed as 'brokers' ...

Thus it calls (ibid., p.198) for 'the development of flexible decentralised patterns of organisation based upon a social care plan which takes full account of informal care, and mobilises voluntary and statutory provision in its support'. This it labels 'community social work'.

The final chapter contains some more detailed comments on informal help and its potential in relation to the practice of social work. A focus on 'caring for the carers' in social work might reduce referrals to social workers through lessening the fragility and vulnerability of informal help (ibid., p.200). The function of social workers emerges as 'to enable, empower, support and encourage, but not usually to take over from, social networks' (ibid., p.209). In particular, social workers are recommended: first, to acquaint themselves, standing 'in their client's shoes', with the personal network of a client and its features; second, to consider how the links deriving from close geographical contact can be developed and added to; third, to keep in mind the development of 'communities of interest' which could provide support and might not be geographically limited (ibid., pp.205-6).

So, social workers are urged to acknowledge that those who form a client's social environment constitute an essential component of the client's welfare. Nevertheless, some significant qualifications are recorded in the Report. People who are vulnerable and 'difficult' can be ostracised or 'scapegoated' by neighbours, even their own kin. Thus it is observed that a focus on informal networks, being 'arenas of conflict between their members as well as sources of social care', will necessitate the involvement of social workers (ibid., pp.212-13):

in decisions not to take action when neighbours and relatives demand it, in intervening when no one in the client's circle wants anything done and in working with people who have totally opposed views as to what would be the best way to solve a problem.

The Report also makes clear that informal caring networks should not be imposed on clients (ibid., p.213), partly for reasons just indicated. Social work, then, retains 'values' of its own. And if, 'in some circumstances', informal carers should have 'direct influence on how resources are used' (ibid., p.214), certain dilemmas still cannot be avoided (ibid., p.216):

Social services departments wishing to promote a community approach to social work have the unenviable task of working out the distribution of their scarce resources between the maintenance of their statutory duties and the support of informal caring networks.

The Committee, however, was not of one mind. In a dissenting note, Pinker argues, amongst other things, that the proposals would leave the most disadvantaged facing a too-large risk of being uncared for; that it is 'a romantic illusion to suppose that by dispersing a handful of professional social workers into local communities we can miraculously revive the sleeping giants of populist altruism' (ibid., pp.244-45);

and that inadequate attention has been paid to the risk of placing in jeopardy the privacy of clients and other citizens. Pinker is probably right to urge a less reckless rush towards sweeping revisions of social work practice. But his position on this should not be confused with a general lack of enthusiasm. He has made it clear in several places elsewhere, that informal welfare should be <u>studied</u> most carefully (1971, 1974 and 1979).

In another dissenting note, three members of the Committee move to the other pole. The call here is for social workers to be much more physically identified with 'neighbourhoods' than is suggested in the main Report. This, they say, is necessary for formal and informal welfare to work well together, for each to be in easy contact with the other. Thus they remark (ibid., p.222):

> Clearly a knowledge of local cultures, problems, thought patterns and structures is important. If the social worker (and his organisation) is ignorant of these, is seen as an outsider coming from the 'welfare' and from another class or type of area, the chances of understanding people and their networks are considerably reduced.

There can be no disagreement with this last point, but there is a problem posed by the profound changes of organisation and <u>modus operandi</u> being urged. It is the same problem as that posed by the not much more modest recommendations of the main Report: we simply do not know enough about informal welfare for such proposals to be well-founded. This will become apparent in the next section.

THE STATE OF KNOWLEDGE

Studies of informal welfare range from those produced, from a social work or other professional or policy-orientated point of view, with the objective of 'improving' professional interventions to those with a relatively abstract interest in the informal, a consequence of reflections on what constitute key questions and appropriate methods in the study of welfare activities as social phenomena.

One important and relatively early study of the first kind was that produced by Collins and Pancoast (1976). Informal welfare was stumbled on by accident in the course of a review of a formal day care service in the USA (ibid., p.7):

> we found that there already were small neighbourhood networks through which many service needs were met informally and naturally. The individuals involved in them took them so much for granted that they hardly recognized them for what they were.

Certain individuals appeared to be central in helping to make arrangements and giving advice; bartenders and hairdressers were the kind of individuals who emerged as 'natural neighbours'. Such was the interest aroused in the researchers that their focus shifted on to the informal help itself. Moreover, they came to feel that 'natural networks offered possibilities for preventive innovation at every level' (ibid., p.11). This, of course, is consonant with what the Barclay Report was to argue later. Collins and Pancoast were, though, more

8

forthright in their criticism of some existing professional dealings with informal care: 'the natural networks were fitted into existing patterns of practice, a procrustean operation obliterating those aspects of natural systems that give them unique value in the total service complex' (ibid., p.55).

Mayer and Timms in their The Client Speaks (1970) found informal welfare important for a slightly different reason. They were seeking to explore how clients felt about social work. Strangely, that had not been taken very seriously before and it is still something of a Cinderella topic [1]. This attempt to enter the client's 'phenomeno-logical world' (ibid., p.8) led them to realise that access to an experience of informal care by clients influenced decisions about when to seek formal help, the expectations they had of such help and the opinion they formed of what was offered.

With the recent growth of research into informal welfare, in the UK and USA especially, there are signs that the research has become more sensitive and sophisticated. Wellman (1981), amongst others, has stressed the importance of considering the wider personal and social contexts in which help is or is not given. The conditions of altruism must become central topics of study, or else 'we declare ahead of time that a set of ties constitutes a "support system"' (ibid., p.172). To believe that there are 'support systems' 'for all seasons' is, in short, to be unrealistic. The potential for ties to be unsupportive as well as supportive should be acknowledged. And, Wellman observes (ibid., p.186):

> Strength is not always a virtue in ties. While there is some evidence that stronger ties (however measured) provide more support, weaker ties often provide more diverse support because they access a greater number and variety of social circles. Strong ties link network members to persons of similar backgrounds who travel in the same social circles as they do, and the more ramified weak ties link them to other, dissimilar, social circles. Where close friends tend to hear about the same things at the same time, weaker ties are the source of novel news. Consequently, such weak ties can be unique channels to new, diverse sources of information, often proving more useful than strong ties in providing information about job openings, homes for sale and the like.

Wellman - and many of the other contributors to Gottlieb (1981) - are in effect suggesting that wide-ranging community-orientated anthropological and sociological studies which adopt a non-simplistic focus on informal caring need to be undertaken before very much in the way of secure policy recommendations can be delivered. The applicability of 'official' definitions of welfare activities and outcomes to informal

---

[1] The Seebohm Committee found itself unable to sound consumer reaction to the services in any systematic fashion (1968, p.21). And the Barclay Committee did not, though it would have liked to, commission new research on clients' views of social workers (1982, p.ix). Some of the material available is reviewed in Shaw (1978). Studies by Glampson et al. (1977) and Glastonbury et al. (1973) are referred to and drawn upon below.

caring has constantly to be kept under review and the temptation to focus on certain kinds of help alone resisted. As Wellman reminds us (ibid., p.185):

> overall ties link persons and not specific strands. The link between Jack and Jill encompasses more than just help in carrying a pail of water, and the specific kind of help given should be interpreted in the context of their overall relationship.

The complexities involved in attempting a proper understanding of informal work and in providing well-founded policy proposals have also recently been receiving some attention in articles critical of the Barclay Report (Graycar, Timms, and Allan, each 1983). These contributions have been reviewed elsewhere (Offer, 1984) where it has been suggested that the need for a 'break' with the definitions associated with 'formal' patterns of care has still not received full enough recognition.

To some extent, such recent developments reflect something we feel to be vital: the integration of the 'theoretical' and 'applied' traditions of interest in informal welfare (compare Wenger, 1984; and, especially, Bulmer, 1986 - a book which alas appeared too late for proper consideration here). The analyses by Pinker and others of the general state of 'theoretical' work on welfare and the arguments put forward for more careful notice there to be taken of the informal have been discussed in Offer, 1985b, but some comments must be made here.

A key claim is that the unglossed meanings and 'lay theories' with which people live their lives can differ from 'professional' meanings and theories, and are of crucial significance in accounting for such matters as client dissatisfaction with social work, the unpopularity of certain 'client groups', use and non-use of health services, and the low take-up of certain means-tested benefits. (Note that in connection with low take-up, Reddin (1977, p.66) stresses the need to study 'the "logics" of society'.) Not unreasonably, the expectation is that relevant everyday moral meanings and 'rules' find particularly clear expression in informal welfare arrangements. Informal welfare has thus been gaining prominence as a potential source both for putting some flesh on points about the 'plural' nature of certain concepts in social life and also for accounting for certain 'problems' in the 'welfare state'. The task now is to show how the study of informal welfare may best be advanced assuming, as we think one must, that the arguments pointing to the 'theoretical' significance of it are well-founded and that more knowledge is needed, both for the guidance of social work practice and for constructive evaluation of policy proposals.

Sociology and social anthropology promise most in meeting the need for a better picture of the logics and dynamics of informal welfare. In saying this we are aware of having to urge not just developments in the sociology of welfare but also the development of it (and of course the focus on 'welfare' would have to be handled carefully). Indeed, the dearth of welfare studies of an explicitly sociological character has produced serious flaws in the usual academic discourse about welfare (see Carrier and Kendall, 1973; and also Offer, 1985a and 1985b). Perhaps a useful way of distinguishing the sociology of welfare from social administration as a subject is to say that the sociology of welfare is concerned with welfare relations as social relations, rather than as welfare relations.

There is, in fact, a need for a sophisticated sociological approach to be adopted generally when informal welfare is under consideration, whether in research or in the sociology or social policy which is taught in social work training courses. Some discussion of Robinson's _In Worlds Apart_ (1978) may be helpful at this stage both generally and by indicating the particular bearing of a proper sociological sensitivity towards everyday ideas and practices of welfare on the study of interactions between clients and social workers.

According to Robinson, such research as has been conducted into clients has too often been shaped by the definitions of the professionals. However, once such 'moral absolutism' is transcended, the way is open to seeing, what he contends to be the case, that 'one of the major factors lying behind "troubles" in professional-client relationships is the encapsulation of each in sharply differing subjective worlds' (ibid., p.2). Robinson argues, then, that sociologists must recognise that there are or can be multiple realities for the participants in interactions between clients and professionals. These 'multiple realities' may be detected over at least seven matters: the central feature of a problem; the meaning of time scales; the nature of what is trivial and what is serious; the adequacy of information and advice; the evaluation of costs; the meaning of the terms in which prognoses are made; and the nature of 'progress' (see ibid., p.42). More work is, of course, required on such topics, but it must be clear even at this stage that to attempt an adequate understanding of client satisfactions and dissatisfactions is a complex task. On dissatisfactions Robinson observes that 'whether they are "true" from some outside point of view or from the professional's point of view is not the point', and adds that because they reflect the way things look from the client's point of view they will affect his relationship with the services (ibid., p.16).

It is, of course, important not to exaggerate the extent of the discrepancies of meanings either between different types of client or between clients and social workers. But, from their very existence, a further question arises - how to account for them. Thus, as far as clients or 'potential' clients are concerned, Robinson emphasises the formative impact of a whole range of experiences, which includes the informal welfare they have encountered (ibid., p.47):

> People rarely seem to make sense of their problems or their encounters with professionals wholly on their own. Before, during or afterwards they may consult other lay people so that there is, in a sense, a filter between the professional and his client even when they meet one-to-one.

And the definitions and 'rules' affecting 'problems' and such matters as what care and from whom which live at this level need to be taken not as given but as the result of, speaking literally, social work - as the outcome, and not a final one, of the 'negotiations' of the language users in question. The question of why some definitions and rules rather than others appear is an important one for what is really the sociology of morals to pursue (see Pinker, 1976; and Offer, 1984 and 1985b).

11

There are parallel stories to tell about how professionals acquire their perspectives through the processes of training, and how such perspectives are reinforced, embellished or modified by certain features of agency life. Certainly, newly-recruited social workers have the opportunity to learn and deploy professional 'folk' wisdom. Deacon and Bartley express some of what can happen in training courses rather helpfully if a little bluntly (1975, p.69; compare Dingwall's 1978 study of the training of health visitors):

> A social work training course is a setting in which students ... are socialised into becoming a certain type of professional person, taught to think in a particular way and to use an often confused collection of social work maxims, and come to accept, if often with cynical reservation, that they are members of a new profession ...

Robinson's book thus serves to indicate both the sort of dimensions of informal welfare to which we are trying to draw attention, which seem to be too often unacknowledged, and the wider illumination which follows when they are taken on board. The more we discover about informal welfare the better we shall be placed to appreciate some aspects of social work activities.

Similar points have been made by Dingwall (1976) in the context of health and illness. Thus he argues (ibid., p.25):

> medical sociology has failed to develop any conception of illness as a social phenomenon. Clinicians' accounts have been taken over in a relatively uncritical fashion. Since these bear no known relationship to the experience of sick people, they cannot advance our understanding of illness as social conduct.

In order to understand such aspects of illness behaviour as when people decide to make use of 'official' medical services, the lay definitions and 'recipe knowledge' have to be studied on their own terms. Hence, says Dingwall (ibid., pp. 26-7):

> A prime task of the medical sociologist is... the study of how both lay persons and 'professionals' theorise about the human body and its operations and management. From the point of view of the sociologist, all such theories have an equal epistemological status. Taken in context they are all equally sensible, rational and reasonable.

Williams' (1983) Scottish study is an example of research into lay concepts of health which reflects this kind of perspective.

It may be useful to add at this point that one helpful 'method' for furthering the grasp of everyday welfare ideas, and also practices, is the reconsideration of some of the community studies undertaken by both sociologists and social anthropologists (compare Warren, 1981). Of course, many are dated, and, in most, aspects of informal welfare were but a subsidiary interest. Nonetheless, there would seem to be worthwhile returns to be had: for, drawing upon such studies, Julia Parker could observe (1975, pp.26-7):

The long-established, stable communities such as are, or were, found in Bethnal Green, in the mining districts of England and Wales, and in some country areas where families and individuals are bound together by kinship, common residence and often common occupation, develop elaborate 'private' welfare systems based on mutual help and support and are often relatively independent of and resistant to public services.

As was indicated earlier in this section, however, there has been a burgeoning of research studies on informal welfare in recent years, and these often display considerable progress towards the sensitive and sophisticated approach which we feel is necessary. A great deal of this research has been assessed perceptively in Parker, 1985, on which some comments must now be made. As a general observation, Parker says that policies towards informal welfare (ibid., p.6) 'are being developed with very little information about their impact on those who actually do the work of caring from day to day'. However, she indicates that some aspects of informal welfare are better researched than others. The care of elderly and disabled adults and children has been studied relatively often, whilst the rearing of 'normal' children has not. And it has emerged that <u>neighbours</u> are seldom significantly engaged in caring for the heavily dependent, though there may be considerable help from this source over everyday tasks, such as shopping (see Leat, 1983). But the expectations, preferences and problems of both cared-for and carers (especially) have not been adequately studied.

Parker points out the rapid increase of the elderly in the population between 1901 and 1981, particularly of women; the increase of divorce and re-marriage; and the actual drop in the birthrate. Informal care of the elderly, in particular, becomes highly problematic in the future: more elderly, thus more heavily dependent, and fewer 'children' available as carers, with their 'responsibilities' often made complex and perhaps lessened through divorce and re-marriage. Parker reports that no clear evidence has emerged that women's increased participation in the workplace is leading to a withdrawal from informal care by them (and women clearly undertake the bulk of caring). She also records that estimates of people living at home who require care are less than clear. Estimates varying between one and two million have been made.

Parker also considers our knowledge of carers. Care within the family remains a feature of social life (ibid., p. 21): 'One of the most persistent misconceptions about "modern society" is that the family no longer cares for its dependants, especially the elderly'.

However, 'shared care' between family members is uncommon, other relatives withdraw once a main carer has been identified (this, in particular, is something our research confirms). Some evidence has emerged that women are less committed than men to seeing informal care, as opposed to, for example, day care centres, as the preferred care pattern in most specified care situations (see West, 1984). This, presumably, reflects the evidence that care burdens mostly fall on women (Parker notes that, in the context of caring for elderly relatives, Nissel and Bonnerjea found that, ibid., p.31: 'husbands rarely gave direct help to their wives with the care of the dependent relative living with them, even where the wife was employed outside the home'.

We need more knowledge, says Parker, on a range of issues. In particular, we need to know more about the cultural factors which shape carers' expectations of from whom they should get help and what sort of help (including 'outside' help from formal agencies). We also need to find ways of measuring the care that is given; and the costs involved - economic costs, physical costs, emotional costs, and opportunity costs. Our study tries to contribute to answering some of these questions as well as others in a distinctive way - by investigating caring activities and their meanings for the participants through locating them in their social setting. In a context in which policy goals are perhaps being developed ahead of our knowledge we agree with Parker's concluding words (ibid., p.92):

> Above all we need to be sure that the aims of policies encouraging family and community care are concurrent with the opinions and attitudes of the population who will actually be carrying out and/or receiving that care.

Our hope is that we are both contributing towards reaching that still distant goal, as well as supporting an increase in the 'theoretical' significance of the topic of informal welfare.

INFORMAL WELFARE AND SOCIAL POLICY : SOME COMMENTS ON FUTURE PROSPECTS

In this final section we want to comment briefly on how the relationship between government thinking and action and informal welfare may develop in the next few years.

It would not seem very likely that a government would embark on a sudden programme of changes to make statutory social services merely a safety net - putting all burdens primarily on informal care and the private market, thus giving complete expression to what in Catholic circles is sometimes called the principle of subsidiarity (for a discussion see Leaper, 1975). Certainly, on the basis of a piece of relevant research reported by Steiner, such a move would appear ill-advised. The research concerned Clermont County, Ohio, a rural community just east of Cincinnati, with a population of 87,000. Here all general relief was cut off in April 1961, because of financial difficulties. Steiner notes (1966, p.9):

> Clients did not magically become self-sufficient nor did responsible relatives come out of the woodwork when the pressure became intense. Instead, the burden of support was shifted from the public fisc to landlords, grocers, physicians, churches, schools and other civic groups. A study of the aftermath of terminating relief showed a 54 per cent increase in money owed to landlords, grocers, physicians and hospitals during a 15 month period. The sheriff's office reported an increase in the number of evictions, and voluntary agencies such as the Salvation Army reported a rise in requests for aid. Recipients were not newcomers, adrift in a strange place without the likelihood of family attachment in the vicinity.

A more realistic possibility is that there will emerge a piecemeal 'strategy' of chipping away at statutory welfare provision, coupled perhaps with recommendations that it should take informal welfare more into account - with the belief that informal welfare is also going to be, or can be, reinvigorated. And, as Parker, 1985, has suggested, this may increasingly involve an emphasis which shifts away from services having some focus on supporting informal carers to informal carers being seen as a substitute for formal service provision. (Parker also reports studies of recent 'experiments' involving attempts to support informal carers by changes in service provision, particularly in Kent (ibid., ch. 4). Such experiments are continuing and are clearly very important). It must be remembered, though, that, given a genuine desire to see 'needs' being met, more must be known than is at present about the wishes of carers and cared-for regarding 'formal' help, and about 'the conditions of populist altruism' (on this notion see Pinker, 1979). (More attention needs to be paid to relationships between private market care and informal care). Indeed, the wisest course of action in the near future would seem to be to discourage dramatic changes at the levels of policy and provision; though government could certainly consider some changes in social security provision which might help to support informal care: more help to those undertaking care of the chronically sick, for instance, since - as Hadley and Hatch observe (1981, p.91) - 'the provision of almost all informal care in the community relies to some degree on the support of the social security system'.

However, the primary needs at present are, for much more research (including carefully monitored 'experiments' in patterns of service delivery), and for the education of social workers, for instance, to place a sensitive stress on informal care. For in any essentially uninformed programme designed to 'tap' informal care, there is the risk it will either collapse or be driven underground, once domination or appropriation is felt to be being exercised. Yet such a 'colonisation' approach, as Abrams, 1980 termed it, may sometimes be unavoidable, however much we come to know about informal welfare, unless social workers and others are prepared to condone such things as racial prejudice which may be present in informal networks of care and which transgress customary professional values. A similar risk is that discrimination by social workers and others in favour of supporting male carers may continue unnoticed - a risk, identified, for example, in a study of both males and females who were caring for elderly people (Charlesworth et al., 1984, p.35).

The rest of our book reports on our study of informal welfare in a small town in Northern Ireland.[1] For the reasons discussed above we felt it important to study relationships in which informal welfare help took place not just as caring relationships but as social relationships, and this of course had implications for the kind of research approach to be adopted. Thus the result is we hope, a picture of the social context which helps to account for the kind of giving and receiving of help which takes place (or fails to take place). This picture is intended very much to be a contribution to the sociology of welfare, and to the development of it, as well as to debates about social policy and informal welfare.

---

[1] For the original full report see Cecil, Offer and St. Leger, 1985.

2 Studying Glengow

In the previous chapter we considered the 'geographically neutral' reasons for undertaking research into informal welfare. In particular, we argued for a study which gave close attention to the participants' own experience and understandings. That is why our discussion often displays an 'ethnographic' style of presentation, where the material is intended to speak for itself.

There was no special reason for choosing to do the research in Northern Ireland over and above convenience for the researchers involved. The topic, though, had not been studied there, or, indeed, in the Republic of Ireland. And whilst the similarities between Northern Ireland and the rest of the United Kingdom are such that comparison with studies undertaken there is possible, the differences meant that new aspects might emerge, thus enhancing the understanding of informal welfare overall. We knew of no exact precedent for this kind of research. It seemed prudent, therefore, to select a relatively small geographical community which evoked a sense of belonging in the minds of the inhabitants. Of course such a community could probably have been found in an urban setting; but we selected a rural setting - such settings are typical of life for many people in Northern Ireland. We elected to study a community in Northern Ireland which is relatively unaffected by what are sometimes called 'the troubles'. Contrary to a view often held outside the Province, such communities are not uncommon. It was, therefore, mainly for its typicality that we chose a small town in an untroubled rural area. We also felt that a 'troubled' area might prove difficult to study using an ethnographic approach in which we needed to gain the confidence of people. We chose, moreover, to study a 'mixed' community where Protestants predominate, as they do in Northern Ireland as a whole. A community in which Catholics were the majority or near majority would have been less typical - at least of the demography of the area of the study. These decisions were taken to maximise the chances of success and usefulness of a project with an untried approach, given the topic concerned.

The area on which this research is based consists of Glengow and its hinterland. The name 'Glengow' is a pseudonym used to disguise the town's identity. Likewise the people mentioned are not referred to by their real names. Glengow is a small Plantation town in a woodland setting in a district which abounds in dolmens, burial chambers and standing stones. In physical appearance Glengow is typical of many small Irish towns. It has a long and wide main street along which are shops, pubs, and houses. Behind the main street lie eight public housing estates. The oldest of these estates was built in 1950; the newest, built in 1980, is still being enlarged – nine more houses are currently due to be built. The town itself, as already indicated, is largely Protestant with over two thirds of its population of twelve hundred being Protestant. To the east of Glengow lies good farming land with a scattered and mainly Protestant population: this region we call Cullydown. To the west, the land becomes quite hilly, even mountainous. The southern part of the hilly area, Ballyreagh, is almost totally Catholic, as is the northern part, Killyullin. Between these two areas lies Magherahill where a scattered community of Presbyterian hill farmers live. This settlement pattern, with Protestants residing in the town and on the good arable land and Catholics in the mountainous region, is fairly typical of towns founded during the period of the Plantation. Plantation towns were established during the early seventeenth century when large numbers of English and Scottish settlers migrated to Ulster. It is a matter of some debate among contemporary historians as to whether the common settlement pattern associated with these towns was the result of a government scheme or whether, as Robinson (1984) and others argue, it arose spontaneously due to eco-logical and cultural factors. (On the general history of Ireland see Lyons, 1973).

The rural population around Glengow is predominantly a scattered one. However, there are three rural housing estates, in Ballyreagh, in Killyullin, and in Cullydown. The area covered in the research extends from the town for a distance of some eight miles in the Ballyreagh direction, five or so miles out to Killyullin and Magherahill, and four miles to the east of the town. The population of Glengow is gradually increasing; some of the increase comes from the migration of people from the surrounding rural areas to the town. A number of the immigrants to the town have moved into public housing provided by the Housing Executive.[1] There has also been an increase in private property building, including a small private estate to the south of the town.

The most substantial single employer in the town is an engineering works. It is not, however, particularly significant in terms of offering local employment. Of the 73 workers employed, 32 are local, that is from within a five mile radius of Glengow. The number of workers employed here has declined over the last five years. Other smaller engineering firms in the vicinity also offer some employment. The unemployment rate in Glengow is typical of Northern Ireland as a whole, currently running at over 20 per cent. Nearly a quarter of male household heads in our sample were unemployed. Most of the employed male household heads worked full-time, whereas of the women who were in employment approximately half worked part-time only.

---

[1] The Northern Ireland Housing Executive is a non-elected body, responsible for public housing throughout Northern Ireland.

The class structure of Glengow is not easy to analyse and present. In general the class structure in Northern Ireland is different from England. Not only are the patterns of land ownership and the range of occupations rather different in the two countries, but a number of the indicators, which in England so readily identify class position, are missing or have different meanings attributed to them. However, in order to present a very general picture of the social stratification of the area, we have used that standard basis of social class classification, the Registrar-General's list of occupations. We have modified it slightly in order to place the large number of farmers in our sample in a category of their own. In general in Glengow, social stratification and its effects are best understood in terms of a range of factors in addition to occupation, especially standard of living and social intercourse. In other words both class and status are considered to be important. In terms of our modified version of the Registrar-General's classification, the social class distribution was as set out in Table 1.

Table 1   Social Class In Glengow

Registrar-General's Category	Male Head of Household	Female Head of Household
I	8	0
II	26	24
Farmer	16	1
III non-manual	5	25
III manual	40	7
IV	21	38
V	8	14
Never worked	3	37
	127	146

Of male heads 31 per cent were professional, semi-professional, business or clerical people; 13 per cent were farmers, 32 per cent skilled manual and 23 per cent semi-skilled or unskilled. This indicates a marked middle-class presence, if, following the Registrar-General, farmers are included in that category. Women, as is usual, tend to be bunched in the semi-professional (and business), clerical/ secretarial and semi-skilled and unskilled categories.

An alternative classification would broadly embrace the following categories:

(1) well-to-do professionals, comprising those in the Registrar-General's first category, such as doctors, clergy, large well-established farmers and businessmen;

(2) generally those who are middle class, including teachers, nurses and health visitors, small or medium businessmen, such as publicans and shopkeepers and most farmers;

18

(3) skilled manual workers in stable employment and enjoying a good standard of living;

(4) skilled workers excluding the above, and semi-skilled and unskilled workers, and very small farmers.

These categories are very approximate. Generally classes one and four are fairly clearly set apart from other classes, but the boundary between classes two and three in particular is blurred, and intermarriage is not uncommon (see McCafferty 1985).

The main Protestant denominations in Northern Ireland are Presbyterian, Church of Ireland and Methodism; smaller sects are the Baptists, Brethren, Congregationalists, and Free Presbyterians. In Glengow, there are two Presbyterian churches and a Church of Ireland church in the town (there is also a Free Presbyterian church whose congregation is largely drawn from outside Glengow). The Catholic chapels lie outside the town, one in Ballyreagh and one in Killyullin. As has already been noted, Glengow is situated in a quiet area that is little affected nowadays by 'the troubles'. Although there have been a couple of violent incidents in recent years, the underlying sectarian tension that is undoubtedly present rarely surfaces except around the twelfth of July. Catholics and Protestants within the town get on reasonably well; however, the Catholics of Killyullin and particularly of Ballyreagh are viewed in a different light by the town Protestants. These two areas are referred to by them as 'bandit country' and would be rarely visited. The town Catholics do not draw a distinction between themselves and the people of Ballyreagh and Killyullin; they regularly go to these areas to attend chapel and have kin ties that span these three areas. Of the five clergymen, the elder of the two Presbyterian Ministers plays the most prominent role within the community. He had been on the district council for a number of years. He was described as being 'Mr Glengow' and as having a finger in every pie. Certainly a number of people, both Catholic and Protestant, go to him for advice and assistance. The different roles that the five clergy play within the community may be due to a variety of factors, such as, the contrasting nature of the relationship of a Catholic priest to his congregation on the one hand and that of a Protestant minister on the other (see Harris, 1961); the geographical localities served by the clergy, which are in some cases overlapping and in some cases distinct; the fact of working in a mixed community, which may affect the nature of a clergyman's work; and, finally, the personalities of the five men. One clergyman in particular is a very gentle man who is noted for his visiting of the sick, and is extremely popular amongst his congregation. The role of the clergy in the care of the sick is largely limited to offering affective support to the carer and the cared-for. Limited as this service is, it is greatly valued. In situations in which it was not forthcoming a desire for contact with the clergy was sometimes expressed. In one case considerable animosity was felt towards a clergyman by the mother of a disabled child because he did not visit her and her child, although they were members of his congregation.

Glengow is not very big, yet it is still of considerable social and commercial importance for the surrounding area, even though this importance has diminished over the years. It used to be a thriving market town and its wide main street attests to this. On a Saturday night the shops would remain open until ten o'clock at night and it would be very busy. Good roads connect Glengow to the larger towns in the vicinity. The largest town, Farreaghly, is some dozen miles to the north. Like many such places Glengow has become less accessible by public transport than formerly through the loss of a railway. Glengow lost its admittedly paltry service as long ago as 1950, although the station building still stands. The bus service to and from the town is rather poor. However, a large number of people own a car. People from Glengow do not consider themselves to be living in a remote or inaccessible situation; many travel in to Farreaghly regularly for work, or to shop or make use of the other amenities there. In contrast, people from Farreaghly consider Glengow and other towns of a similar size in the area to be rather remote and describe them as being 'up country'.

But while Glengow has indeed lost some of its commercial importance it remains a reasonably busy centre. As well as a number of grocery shops the town also has: two hardware stores; a drapery store; two chemist shops; two hairdressers; two banks; a post office; a sweetshop and newsagent; three garages; a shoe shop; an electrical goods store; two cafes and two take-aways; a butcher; a greengrocer; and, most recently, a video shop. Glengow also boasts five pubs and a library. Milk, bread and grocery vans and a mobile library unit service the rural areas.

Glengow's more enduring social significance within the surrounding countryside lies partly in the number of organisations that exist, and the number of events which take place, in the town. As in most small towns in Northern Ireland many activities are associated with the churches: for example, there are regular meetings of the Presbyterian Women's Association, and of the Mothers' Union. For children there is the Boys' Brigade, as well as the Junior Christian Endeavour. Badminton and bowls are played in the Presbyterian church hall, while in the parish hall in Killyullin there is a regular bingo night. A number of events, while not directly associated with the different churches, are nevertheless divided along the main religious boundary. The involvement of some people with either a loyalist band or a nationalist band as well as the playing of sport is thus divided in this way. However, these associations are not necessarily based in the town itself.

The Women's Institute (WI) is an organisation with a membership of over sixty, of which the vast majority are Protestant. It is, however, avowedly a non-sectarian organization; indeed the Glengow branch of the WI was co-founded many years ago by a Catholic woman. That it is predominantly Protestant reflects the largely urban and middle-class character of the membership. Admittedly, it does hold its meetings in the British Legion Hall which might deter the attendance of some nationalists. However, Glengow is lacking in a neutral site for community activities, as are many small towns. Consequently a range of activities takes place in the hall. The Young Farmers' Club (YFC) offers various structured activities for young people. The events which take place at YFC meetings, which are also held in the British Legion hall, are largely based on competitive games. The YFC has a mainly middle-class and Protestant membership. The youth club at the far end of the town is used predominantly by working-class young people of both religions and its activities are less structured than those at the YFC.

Before reviewing the social and welfare services in Glengow, it is necessary to summarise the distinctive integrated organisation of health and social services in Northern Ireland. Since the re-organisation of local government services in 1973, the personal social services have been placed together with the health services under four, non-elected

20

Health and Social Services Area Boards - namely, Northern, Southern, Eastern, and Western. Each Board has the task of providing a full range of both health and social services within a designated area of Northern Ireland, and they act together on certain matters of common concern through a central services agency and staff council. The areas are divided into units of management. Delivery of social, medical, and nursing services is co-ordinated at this level by an executive team (for more on the Area Boards in general see Birrell and Williamson 1983). The Northern Area Board is divided into four districts: Glengow falls into the sub-district of Farreaghly. Social work fieldwork services in Farreaghly sub-district are delivered by an intake team plus three care teams and a mental handicap team. These teams operate throughout the whole sub-district and not on a patch basis. All work coming into the social work office in Farreaghly is channelled through the intake team. It is either dealt with directly, if it is of a short term nature, or it is assessed and passed to a care team if it is likely to involve long term work. The three care teams are: the family care team which is responsible for long term family casework, 'at risk' child care interventions, children taken or received into care, fostering, adoption, and wardship work; the community care team, which is responsible for services to the elderly and the physically handicapped; and the health care team which is responsible for the elderly and services to the hospitals. The home help service is organised by social work assistants operating on a patch basis. The sub-district is divided for this purpose into two areas, each one worked by a group of social work assistants.

As Glengow is not part of a 'patch' system the nearest social work office is twelve miles away in Farreaghly. Consequently, social workers are not a familiar sight for the people of Glengow, unlike the doctors and the police. Social workers in the Farreaghly office describe the social services as being 'inaccessible' to people in Glengow. A number of cases which in Farreaghly would be referred on to social workers, are dealt with in Glengow by those professionals on the spot, namely the police and the doctors. Most of the referrals which are made to the social work team come from doctors and the police; some come from the community - both self-referrals and from people telephoning on someone else's behalf.

The social workers responsible for the Glengow area say they try to identify and make use of informal networks of support which are, they add, 'almost exclusively family'. As far as care from neighbours is concerned they say that 'Glengow is not outstanding on the basis of good neighbourliness...it is not a particularly caring community'. They feel that although it is difficult to detect any significant differences between informal care in rural and in 'urban' Glengow, a greater number of their cases come from the town than from the country area which might suggest a more adequate support system in the rural area than in the town. One social worker, a resident of the town, had gained the impression that the people of Ballyreagh were more mutually supportive than people elsewhere in the region. This is likely to be associated with the extensive family ties in this area.

Home helps are employed by the Health and Social Services Board and as such are clearly agents of formal care. Yet the role of the home help can be viewed as straddling the boundary between formal and informal care. The 'informal' aspect of their care-giving role arises from the fact that a home help usually works within her own neighbourhood. In many cases she is likely to have known her client prior to working as a home help. It is not unusual for a home help to begin her career through the specific request for help from an elderly neighbour. We have one example from our case studies of a woman whose role of home help arose directly from her unpaid involvement in the care of an elderly neighbour over a number of years. Virtually every home help interviewed admitted to working beyond the time allocated and for which they are paid. Thus, as well as their role as paid carer, a large number of home helps also take on the role of an unpaid neighbour-carer, for a few hours a week at least. So home helps, in some circumstances, fill the role of good neighbour and, as we will see, the 'good neighbour' is highly esteemed in Glengow. In fact, though, home helps are viewed somewhat ambivalently in Glengow. A number of people expressed the view that home helps are lazy, and, more significantly, that they should not get paid for the work that they do. Thus while home helps form part of the relatively small group of people who are actually 'neighbouring' in Glengow, their virtue in doing so is tainted in the eyes of a number of people because they get paid for their labour. It is felt that they should do the work that they do for nothing, just 'out of neighbourliness'. This opinion is, perhaps, felt and expressed because of the fact that all the home helps are women, and the role of women in this society is largely a domestic family-centred caring one. For many people, women do not have a recognised place in the market economy.

A number of home helps deal with the social services on behalf of their client. For example, one woman wrote to the Supplementary Benefit office on behalf of her illiterate client who had very few possessions. She succeeded in acquiring for him £200 with which to buy bedding and clothing.

Various voluntary organisations exist in the area. Some of these are associated with a church. St Vincent de Paul is attached to the Catholic church in Killyullin and is composed of twelve members, all men. There are about six or seven people in the area considered by them to be 'needy', who are visited by two of the members every week. These are mainly elderly people. Their 'need' may not be financial, although when it is the society will 'put the welfare on to them'. The main need of some elderly people is for company as they are lonely, and the society responds to that. Members of the society also visit the hospitals every week because at any one time there is likely to be someone from the parish in hospital. Both Catholics and Protestants are served by the society.

There are three Senior Citizens clubs in the area. The club in Killyullin, for example, organises three functions: a summer outing; a Christmas dinner held either in the church hall or in the hotel in the town; and an event at Hallowe'en. These events are in part funded by the social services. The Senior Citizens club in the town had initially been run on a voluntary basis. A meal and entertainment were provided on a regular basis for elderly people who were collected by volunteer car drivers. Money was raised for the various events by the holding of cake sales, treasure hunts and so forth. After about three years social workers became involved in the running of the club. This appears to have resulted in a sharp decline in the level of local interest and involvement in it. The original organiser ceased, after a time, to continue working with the group.

For young people there is a youth club. It has, as already indicated, a predominantly working class membership. Approximately two-thirds of its membership of sixty or so are Protestant, which indeed reflects the proportion of Protestants to Catholics in the town. Three times as many boys as girls attend the club. Activities at the club include repairing toys for Dr. Barnardo's homes as well as the usual run of sports and games.

The Gateway Club for the mentally handicapped was started up about nine years ago in Glengow. It arose out of the need felt by members of the Parents Association of the special care school for social activities for the mentally handicapped. There is some overlap between the youth club and the Gateway Club with members of one club occasionally attending the other. This is at least partially because the leader of the youth club is also the organiser of the Gateway Club. Other voluntary groups in the town include the Red Cross, a playgroup, and the British Legion.

There are twelve full-time and three part-time policemen stationed in the police barracks in Glengow. The police sergeant describes Glengow as being a place that is little affected by the 'troubles' - 'an area where we can police virtually as normal'. The main duties of the police are to do with road traffic accidents, crimes such as burglary, and family rows. The police play a role in the care of the community both directly, by dealing on the spot with situations which might otherwise be dealt with by social workers, and indirectly, by liaising with other statutory bodies such as the Housing Executive on behalf of members of the community. The sergeant felt that in Glengow 'people would be friendly towards each other; there are never any instances of people being neglected. If neighbours know that (old people) are in difficulty they will certainly help or come and tell us'. This perhaps indicates a somewhat different assessment of caring in Glengow to that expressed by the social workers.

A later chapter examines Glengow as a neighbourhood and suggests that while the shared ideology of 'neighbourliness' does reflect actual neighbourly activities, these activities are of a limited nature which rarely extend to what Bell (1979) refers to as 'dedicated involvement' or what we are describing as 'informal welfare'. Here we give some examples of the activities of people in Glengow, not in order to discuss the concept of neighbourliness but solely to illustrate aspects of daily life in the area. People in Glengow meet in a variety of settings. Not only are there the various organisations which have been mentioned, but people meet informally in the street, in bars, collecting children from school, and so on. People also meet in the course of their work. For example, farmers may meet at one of the local livestock markets, as well as having contact through the occasional lending of farm implements and labour. However, some people from the outlying areas might become rather isolated were it not for various events which serve to bring people together. Occasions such as funerals and wakes may involve a wide range of people. The custom of 'stations', whereby the priest holds a Mass in one house in each townland during Lent and October, also draws people together who in a sparsely populated area might only occasionally have cause to meet. In preparation for the station the women from the other Catholic households in the townland go to the house in which Mass is to be held and thoroughly clean it, and bring with them cutlery and crockery, and cakes and sandwiches. After Mass everyone stays for tea and to talk and tell stories.

23

Ceilidhing still takes place although with less frequency than in the past. Other visiting between neighbours occurs, and we know of old people who are regularly visited by some of their neighbours; one elderly man has a number of visitors, some of whom come bearing small gifts.

The contact which people have with one another may be a function of their social or occupational role. For example, the postman is in contact with people who may otherwise be quite isolated. Not only is contact made with the postman himself, but he is also the deliverer of items of local news and verbal messages between people. It may be an indication of the importance of the postman that he does not need to take any lunch with him to work, for he always gets fed at some of the houses which he visits. The function of some roles may be changing - for whereas the priest felt that people go to him for comfort and advice as much as they ever did, the doctor felt that he was consulted rather less nowadays on extra-medical matters such as social and marital problems.

The nature of contact between people inevitably reflects the nature of the community. Moreover, the contact and involvement which men have with their neighbours will differ from that which women have. Women are commonly brought into contact with one another through their maternal role, and to a limited extent childcare gets shared among some groups of women.

Relations between neighbours are not, of course, always good. We know of next-door neighbours who were not on speaking terms for a number of years, and cases where aid, which could have been offered, was withheld. On the other hand, neighbourly aid might be offered only to be rejected. An interesting example of such a case concerns a girl who was suffering from a serious disease whose mother wanted to take her to Lourdes. Her mother collected money from people in the neighbourhood, who gave generously, so that her daughter might be able to go. However, the girl's father was angry when he learnt of the collection and insisted that all the money be given back as he could afford to pay for his daughter's pilgrimage himself.

Having explained our reasons for choosing Glengow as the site for our research, and indicated the kind of town it is, we now proceed to an account of our involvement with Glengow, and the methods which we employed to collect data. A slightly unusual feature of this research, given some orientation towards policy considerations, and that funding came primarily from a government department, was that an extended period of participant observation ran concurrently with more formal methods of data collection. This involved the Research Fellow moving into Glengow in September, 1983. She initially lived in a flat in the main street of the town then moved to a house on a rural estate three miles out. Gaining entrance into the community was helped by the presence in Glengow of a couple of people who had connections with the researchers and the university.

She did not attempt to conceal her role as a researcher while endeavouring to participate in the life of the community within the limits set by religious and gender considerations. She took part in various associational activities, becoming an active member of the Women's Institute and participating in a dressmaking class. As a way of meeting people, and of indicating sectarian neutrality, she attended, at a very early stage of the fieldwork period, one service held by each of the main religious denominations. In practice this meant that she attended four different church services. She decided that it would not be desirable to attend any one church regularly, as although this would have facilitated considerable involvement with members of that particular congregation, it would also have seriously distanced her from members of other churches. In fact on a number of occasions she went to some length to assure people, quite truthfully, that she had no religious affiliation at all. She attended both the main Catholic and Protestant festivals; going to the twelfth of July celebration with Protestant neighbours from Cullydown and to the Ancient Order of Hibernian parade with friends from Ballyreagh.

She became involved in a network of neighbours among whom various activities took place such as babysitting, the lending and borrowing of commodities and also some social events. Her informal contacts were more commonly with women than with men. However, this was not a serious disadvantage since our research has found that the bulk of care is given by women, within the domestic sphere. Indeed, a greater understanding of the lives of women proved valuable. Attempts to broaden the range of social contacts by, for example, going drinking in local pubs were only partially successful. Unlike a male fieldworker it was not possible nor desirable for the Research Fellow to sit alone in a bar in order to participate in the local talk. She was at first dependent upon friends from outside Glengow to accompany her to bars, only later did she occasionally go out drinking with local people.

It is not possible to mix equally with all social groups in Glengow, nor indeed in any other town. Many internal divisions cross-cut the community; religion, class, and gender being just the most obvious ones. The Research Fellow deliberately did not align herself with any one specific category of people, and consequently paid the price of not being deeply involved with any of them. Instead she interacted with Protestants and Catholics - urban and rural, middle class and working class.

A theme relevant to the research was the use of the common terms of address and reference within the family as an indication of familial relations of power, status and affection, (see Firth et al., 1969). The Research Fellow made use of her contacts within the Women's Institute to administer twenty questionnaires to its members. These, along with information acquired through her period of fieldwork, provided the data for the discussion on kin terminology in chapter 3 on the family.

Interviews were conducted with people, from both within and without Glengow, whom it was felt had some particular knowledge of the community which would be of value to our study. The following people were thus contacted: clergymen; headteachers; general practioners; a local councillor; the president of the local St. Vincent de Paul society; the leader of the local youth club, who was also involved in a club for the mentally handicapped; a teacher in the High School who had amassed an impressive collection of local artefacts of historical and sociological interest; and elderly people who had clear memories and a willingness to talk at length of past events. The police, social workers, and twelve home helps were also interviewed.

Members of 92 households were also interviewed. A questionnaire (see Appendix A) was used which was designed to elicit information on the composition of the respondent's household; the family of the respondent and of the respondent's spouse living outside the household; whether any member of the household or the family was chronically sick or disabled; and the degree of contact, if any, with representatives of various statutory institutions. The first round of these interviews began in November, 1983. While all of these involved the use of a questionnaire, most interviews went on to include a less structured discussion session. Unstructured discussion covered various themes as appropriate, including kinship, friendship, marriage and courtship, life crises, sexual division of domestic labour, membership of organisations, as well as questions on knowledge about, and contact with, social services.

We initially attempted to identify households to interview by drawing a sample of names and addresses from the electoral register. However, this was abandoned when it proved to be largely unworkable as a way of locating and contacting people, particularly those living in the more rural areas. The alternative method used was to visit houses at random while ensuring that all the different regions of the area under study were included. Thus interviews were conducted in all of the housing estates and in the older part of the town, as well as the different rural areas. A small number of people were interviewed because they were relatives or other contacts of people already interviewed. We followed up social and familial connections in this way in order to obtain a picture of the networks in existence in the area, and also to gain a fuller understanding of the situation of the person initially contacted.

While our interest in informal welfare encompassed care within the community in general, we wished to pay special attention to the elderly and disabled adults and children. It was therefore important that a sufficient number of households containing at least one elderly or disabled member was included in the sample. As our sample did not provide us with an adequate number of families with disabled children we contacted the appropriate social work office which provided us with the names and addresses of such families in the area. In order to have a sufficient number of old people in the sample, interviews were conducted with every household on a small estate of bungalows for the elderly. This also provided the opportunity for an intensive study of neighbouring within a very small community.

In January, 1985, it was decided to extend the quantitative coverage of the study by commissioning a survey based on structured interviews. Consequently at Easter, 1985, a further hundred interviews were conducted using a questionnaire slightly modified from that used initially. These interviews were conducted by five interviewers from the Policy Planning Research Unit (PPRU) in Northern Ireland. This survey, which was preceded by a pilot study in a small neighbouring town, was confined to Glengow town itself; that is, no interviews were conducted in the surrounding rural area. The more limited geographical area was chosen primarily in order that a fairly intensive picture of networks be provided.

Fifty of the questionnaires included a question on the role of social workers. The other fifty contained a question which consisted of two vignettes, each of which presented a specific social problem. Respondents were asked, in each case, to say how they would cope with such a problem. The idea of presenting questions in such a form was derived from the work of Glastonbury et al. (1973) and Glampson et al. (1977). The point of using the vignettes was described by Glastonbury et al. as follows (ibid., p.197):

The object was to see how far the respondent would envisage particular social agencies as being helpful in these kinds of circumstances, or conversely how far the problems could either be tackled within the community or be such as to promote feelings of pessimism and powerlessness.

Other questions also elicited information on attitudes to offering and receiving aid.

The PPRU questionnaires were edited at the Unit before being passed on to the research team in Coleraine. Coding of the quantitative data was undertaken mainly by the Health Studies Research Unit at the University, and the material was analysed using an SPSS package (Statistical Package for the Social Sciences).

The numbers involved in the original sample and the PPRU sample of Easter, 1985, and the areas covered, are recorded in Table 2 (p.28). As this Table shows, we conducted interviews throughout the housing estates (certain estates located close to each other have been grouped together here to simplify categorisation) as well as in the old town. In the rural area, both the Catholic and Protestant hill areas as well as the Protestant lowland regions were studied. This was in order to ensure an adequate representation of people of different social groups among our sample.

Some of our respondents were asked to keep a diary in order that we might obtain a profile of social contacts in Glengow. Information on the diarists' social networks was obtained from them, and also on their associational activities, leisure pursuits, and, occasionally, attitudes and feelings. Some information was also obtained on diet and hospitality. Fourteen people from the sample completed a diary. Respondents were asked to keep the diary for a period of two weeks. In one case the diary was kept for three weeks and in another case it was kept for a month. (See Appendices G and H for the instructions on keeping a diary and samples of the design layout.) A respondent would be asked to keep a diary if we were particularly interested in his or her circumstances and required additional information. Respondents were also chosen on the basis of their co-operation during the initial interview(s), and the degree of 'rapport' established between the respondent and the interviewer. We felt that it was essential that the respondent was happy about keeping the diary as it involved a considerable amount of time and effort on his or her part to complete. In all but a few cases the diaries were kept by women (eleven diaries were kept by women and only three by men). This, combined with the fact that the great majority of our respondents in the whole sample were women, meant that the social networks of men were less adequately tapped than those of women. The fullness of the records provided by the diaries varied considerably and there was some evidence that contacts, as well as other activities, were understated. The period of a fortnight was, perhaps, too short to provide a comprehensive picture of a respondent's social networks; for example, in one diary which was kept for over four weeks, none of the three people named elsewhere as 'close friends' appeared. Despite drawbacks the diaries did provide a very useful supplement to the interviews and helped to give greater depth to the picture that we had of the lives of these respondents.

Table 2   The Samples

Number of Households

Glengow town	Original Sample	PPRU Sample	Total

1. Larchwood Gardens
   Beechtree Park
   Elmwood Park
	8	15	23

2. Treetop Park Springdale	18	23	41
3. Hollyberry Drive Oakleaf Gardens	6	19	25
4. Silverbirch Park	7	8	15
5. Main Street area	14	35	49
Total Town	53	100	153

Number of Households

Outside Glengow	Original Sample	PPRU Sample	
6. Ballyreagh	18	---	18
7. Killyullin	5	---	5
8. Magherahill	6	---	6
9. Cullydown	10	---	10
Total Outside Glengow	39		39
Total	92	100	192

In order to analyse data on contact between a respondent and relatives, a contact index was constructed which takes into account face-to-face, telephone and letter contact. See Appendix D for details of this index.

In summary, we employed a number of research methods throughout the project to collect data both of a qualitative and a quantitative nature. The methods used were:

1   eighteen months of participant observation by the Research Fellow

2   questionnaires on kinship terminology

3   interviews with prominent people in the town and with professionals associated with the town

4   structured interviews using a questionnaire conducted by the research team

5   unstructured interviews conducted by the research team based on a questionnaire and followed by further questioning and discussion. A number of these included the use of a tape recorder

6   an additional set of structured interviews conducted by interviewers from an outside research unit

7   diaries kept by a number of people from within the sample.

Thus a range of methods of data collection was used. We felt that no one method would have been adequate to provide the depth and breadth of information which we required. The weaknesses of one method have, it is hoped, been offset by the strengths of another. The complementary nature of the research tools provided us in the end with a good supply of quantitative and qualitative data.

3 The family

This chapter examines the family as a social institution in Glengow. The material presented provides the necessary background for an understanding of care given within the family, the subject of the following chapter. After some comments relating mainly to family size we attempt to distinguish between different types of family-household, to indicate patterns of residence and of marriage, and to discuss gender roles and the ways in which members of families 'define' each other through the terms of address they use.

Some demographic data will give a picture of the basic nature of the family within Northern Ireland, and within Glengow in particular. Family size in Northern Ireland is significantly larger than in the rest of the United Kingdom. Figures given in Regional Trends (1984) show that the average household size in the U.K. as a whole is 2.72, while it is 3.2 in Northern Ireland (figures refer to 1981). The difference between the U.K. as a whole and Northern Ireland is more strikingly illustrated by the figures which show the percentage of households comprising one or more adults with four children under the age of sixteen; the U.K. figure is 1.5 while the figure for Northern Ireland is 5.2. The average size of household for our sample from Glengow is 3.39 (3.26 for Protestant households, and 4.26 for Catholic households). We felt that the Glengow sample was insufficiently large to subdivide the figures in order to assess family size in relation to such other factors as class position or educational attainment, or to take into account parental age in order to place family size within a recent historical context. Many of the younger respondents in the sample would not, presumably, have completed their family at the time of the interview. However, while it was not uncommon for families to contain four, five or six children it was noticeable that a number of our interviewees came from larger families than they themselves produced.

A range of family-household types can be identified in Glengow. Although it is not always easy clearly to distinguish between the types we loosely categorize them as follows:

(i)   Conjugal households. The core of this household type is the married couple, with or without their unmarried children. Husband and wife households, together with husband, wife and children households form the single most numerous group in our sample; 58.3 per cent of our overall sample of households fell into this category. 44.8 per cent consisted of a married couple with their children.

(ii)   Widow/widower households. These are households where the head of the household is a widow or a widower. 17.7 per cent of our sample were of this household type. There is a far greater number of widows than widowers (thirty-one widows and three widowers).

(iii)   Sibling households. Unmarried siblings living together form this household type. The nine cases of sibling households in our sample were divided equally between two brothers; two sisters; and a brother and a sister.

(iv)   Extended households. These consist of a husband and wife and family members other than or as well as their unmarried children. For example, a married child or children with spouse/s as well as their children, if any. Another common type is where an elderly relative lives with the husband and wife.

(v)   Bachelor/spinster/separated/divorced households. This type consists of the never-married and the post-married but excludes widows and widowers and those living in sibling households. The majority of these households are composed of people living alone, but some have children living with them.[1]

Any one family will not, of course, maintain the same form throughout the duration of its existence but will pass through different stages. An obvious example is the family household which initially consists of a newly-married childless couple; then evolves into a family consisting of parents and children; and then reverts to consisting solely of the original married couple, once the children grow up and leave home to marry and create new families of their own. A long-term perspective is needed when looking at family types in order to avoid grouping together seemingly similar cases which are in fact dissimilar. For example, a married couple without children may be in a pre-childbearing stage; a post-childbearing/rearing stage; or be childless through infertility or through choice.

---

[1]   We follow Fox (1978) in this style of family-type categorisation.

PATTERN OF RESIDENCE

A sample from among our respondents indicated that the average age of marriage in Glengow is twenty-three for women and twenty-six for men. The residence pattern in Glengow is predominantly patri-virilocal, that is , it is common for the woman to move upon marriage to be with her husband who will remain in his home town. This residence pattern is likely to have arisen because of the predominantly patrilineal system of inheritance, and in particular the strong tendency for land ownership to be passed down the male line. Thus in the past within the farming community, the newly-wed woman would have left her father's home to live with her husband and her husband's family on their farm. This tendency towards patri-virilocal residence adhered to by the farming and non-farming communities in the area means that a large number of the married women presently living in Glengow originated from outside of the town, moving in upon marriage usually from nearby towns or townlands, although sometimes from further afield. The patri-virilocal residence pattern is a tendency rather than an articulated ideal and is dependent upon a variety of factors, including land ownership, occupation of husband and wife, the availability of accommodation, husband's family size, wife's family size, and inter-familial and intra-familial affectivity.

The pattern of residence within the Glengow area is thus that a married man is likely to live near to his natal family (that is, his family of birth) and a short distance from his affines (that is, his 'in-laws') while a married woman is likely to live near her affines and a short distance from her natal family. However, alongside this tendency towards close residential proximity of kin exists the ever present factor of Irish emigration. It is not uncommon to come across families where most family members live within a distance of some five miles of each other (particularly the male members of the family for the reasons already noted) while a few family members live as far afield as Britain, Canada, Australia or South Africa.

PATTERN OF MARRIAGE

There is little inter-marriage between the two main religious groupings in Glengow, as in Northern Ireland as a whole (in other words, they are endogamous). With relatively rare exceptions Catholics marry Catholics and Protestants marry Protestants. While strong opposition to a mixed marriage may be expressed within the families concerned (although this is not always the case) and in extreme cases may lead to intra-familial breaches, opposition from the wider community rarely takes the form of anything other than expressed disapproval and gossip. For some, such disapproval is based on the consideration of the practical problems of living in a divided community. A middle-aged Catholic woman who thought that the frequency of mixed marriages had greatly increased over the last ten years expressed her reservations as follows:

> I think that there are enough problems in married life, ... apart from religion or anything else, that we all meet enough problems in married life by marrying a partner that is the same religion as ourselves ... Here we have so many things cropping up like celebrations about this and celebrations about that ... the twelfth of July ... I always think that at times like that it is bound to make a bit of tension, ... it is bound to create problems.

Disapproval can, however, take (or be considered to take) a more sinister form. When a young man from the town was shot and wounded by gunmen, the most common explanation for the attack, as expressed by local people, was that the man in question was going out with a girl of a different religion from himself. The actual motive for the shooting was never firmly established. It was widely condemned in the town and the view was expressed (at least to the Research Fellow) that it was terrible that one could not go out with whom one liked without such a thing happening.

Even within Protestantism, endogamy is the preferred marriage type for each denomination. However, in practice it is not uncommon for marriages to cross the various Protestant denominational boundaries. It is said that only very strict adherents of a faith would insist upon marriage within the denomination. In cross-denominational marriages it is customary for the wedding to take place within the church of the bride, but for the bride thereafter to become a member of her husband's church, which corresponds to the predominant pattern of patri-virilocal residence. An example of a situation where the customary residence pattern was not to be followed was of a young woman, who was shortly to be married, who stated that her (Presbyterian) fiance would not only be moving into Glengow upon their marriage but would also be joining her in the Church of Ireland. Disapproval was expressed at this by an elderly woman, a member of the Church of Ireland who had been a Presbyterian up until the time of her own marriage, who told the younger woman that she should join the church of her future husband. The tendency for a woman to change to the denomination of her husband is thus expected to supplant any loyalty she might have to the church of her upbringing. Among people whose religious commitment is not strong this tendency may not be so pronounced, for example, a woman from an Anglican family occasionally attends the Church of Ireland and sends her children to the Church of Ireland Sunday school despite her husband being Presbyterian. He is a non-believer who never attends church except for weddings and funerals; had he been an attender then his wife and children would have gone with him to his church.

The family does not appear to play an important part in the initial bringing together of potential marriage partners. Most couples meet through friends or at a social event, such as a dance; few become acquainted with their future spouse through their family. This pattern enables a degree of cross-religious contact that would be unlikely to occur were control of the introduction of potential marriage partners in the hands of the family alone. The increased incidence of mixed marriages may result, at least in part, from the decreasing control of the family over its young persons, and a lessening of authoritarian parenthood.[1]

---

[1] See K.H. Connell, 1962, p.519: 'the downright dictatorship of the parents has vanished ... As bride and groom have assumed the right of choice, there has been a widening of the area within which marriage partners are regularly found'.

The family in Glengow, as in Northern Ireland generally, is a very important institution in social and affective terms. The ratio of divorced to married persons in our sample, as in the whole of Northern Ireland,[1] is relatively low but it is not possible to draw a completely accurate comparison with the rest of the United Kingdom, for while there is less apparent family breakdown in Northern Ireland as expressed in the low divorce rate, the divorce laws differ from those in England, Wales, and in Scotland. While there is a strong sense of family loyalty, and family ties are considered to be very important, there is also a tendency within the society for occasional family feuds to occur, sometimes leading to such breaches within the family that certain family members may not speak to each other for a period of many years. Family feuds are of course not unknown within other societies. It is possible that only those societies in which there exists considerable intensity of feeling about the family produce more than the very occasional family feud.

A further factor to be taken into account when considering the family is that Northern Irish society, outside of Belfast, is predominantly rural; the nature of the family has to be understood within its rural context. The family ties which exist are strongest between parents and children, and these frequently endure well into adulthood. Ties between siblings are not so strong and this is precisely because the primary bond is that between parents and children. Thus, it is recognised that an adult sibling's prime responsibility is to his own children rather than to his siblings. Family ties have a practical as well as an affective content. (The nature and extent of support that is given between family members is the focus of the next chapter). An example of the nature of family ties was given by a male social worker who lives in Killyullin who claimed that 'people here never really leave home'. For eight years whilst living away from home, but before he got married, he returned to his mother's house every weekend, a distance of some twenty-five miles, bringing his washing with him. Similarly a young married woman with two children takes a load of washing to her mother's home every Saturday. In the first case it can be seen that the mother did not cease to be responsible for her son's washing when he left home but only when he married. Up until the time of his marriage he was still considered an integral part of the family-household despite living a considerable distance away for a number of years. Only upon marriage did he come to be seen as detached from his natal family, for at this point he set up a family-household of his own. The responsibility for his washing was then taken on by his wife. In the second case the young woman takes her family-household's washing to do at her mother's home, ostensibly because her mother owns a tumble dryer. However, as the young woman is unhappily married and lonely on the rural housing estate where she lives, the regular contact with her mother is very welcome. The use of her mother's material resources happily coincides with the young woman's need for personal contact. In both cases the responsibility for the washing lies with a woman.

---

[1] The ratio of divorced to married people (i.e. people 'at risk' of divorce) is 1:63.3 in Northern Ireland, compared with 1:18.5 in Britain. Or, to put it another way, there are nearly three and a half times (3.42) as many divorced people in Britain as in Northern Ireland.

When considering family care it is important to identify which member of the family is most likely to take on the main role of carer, and the constraints involved in the 'choice' to do so. Studies so far suggest that the caring role is more commonly undertaken by women than by men (Finch and Groves, 1983; Nissel and Bonnerjea, 1982; Glendinning, 1983; E.O.C., 1982). This section attempts to place the caring role of women in context by considering gender roles within the family and within the wider society of Glengow.

A clear sexual division of labour exists within the family in Glengow. The domestic tasks fall mainly to women, that is, they are largely or solely responsible for cooking, washing up, laundry, ironing, general cleaning of the house, and doing the shopping. Women are also very largely responsible for childcare, although men are more likely to help with childcare than with other tasks that are considered to be the responsibility of women. (See also McCafferty, 1985, whose study of villages in North Antrim and County Londonderry revealed a marked degree of conjugal role segregation). In those situations in which a man has some involvement with domestic tasks it is usually because a woman is unavailable, either temporarily or permanently, to do this work. For example, a man living alone would do a certain amount of domestic labour himself as would a man whose wife was temporarily absent. However, in both types of situations, help from other female kin would probably be forthcoming. Within the home the tasks that a man commonly undertakes are those of changing fuses, plugs and bulbs, mowing the lawn and minor and/or major repairs. In general, women in Glengow are more involved in familial and domestic affairs than are men. A man will defer to his wife over questions concerning domestic issues. A woman's prime role is that which takes place within the home, she is defined by her familial role in a way that a man is not. The association of men with the world that is external to the immediate home, and of women with the domestic realm and the home, is especially apparent among the farming community. Here the care of the stock and the land is the responsibility of the man; women are involved with the running of the farm only to the extent that their main task is to service the men of the family – the farmers. Although a small number of farmers' wives keep fowl this is less common than it was; the boundary between the farm and the farm house is becoming more pronounced especially among the increasing number of farming families who have built and live in a smart new bungalow. Unlike the case of the old style farm house, the farm is left firmly behind at the door of the new bungalow.[1] This association of men with affairs external to the home, and of women with domestic, familial affairs internal to the home may be expressed as follows:

outside:inside::male:female

---

[1] See Hannan and Katsiaouni, 1977, p.26: 'There has been a cumulative withdrawal of the farmer's wife from her farm production role. Either her previous farm tasks have been expanded to a commercial enterprise – e.g., as in pig rearing, milking and poultry keeping – or these enterprises have had to be dropped entirely as profit margins declined and they became uneconomic on a small scale. Hence she is forced to withdraw to the house.'

Such a binary opposition can find expression in a number of forms. Even those domestic tasks which are shared by men and women still have a tendency to fall into this pattern, so that the task of cleaning the car is commonly divided in this way, with the result that the outside of the car is cleaned by the man and the inside is cleaned by the woman. This male-female dichotomy in terms of spheres of primary involvement is an important consideration in the discussion on care within the family where, as will be seen, care takes place within the home and is a private and often a lonely task undertaken largely by women.[1]

Just as the domestic division of labour separates men from women within the realm of daily tasks, so does the social organisation of Glengow separate men from women in other realms of life. Attitudes derived from this bipartite social organisation in turn serve to reinforce it. Pubs in Glengow are predominantly the domain of men; the pub is the place for a man to drink alone or with male friends and to which he might occasionally take his wife or girlfriend. It is rare for a group of women to enter a pub without a male escort and very rare for a woman to go to a pub by herself. The presence of a woman in a pub can have an inhibiting effect on any men present. The situation was reported of a group of men in a pub who were enjoying a long-winded joke which involved a lot of swearing when, at the climax of the joke, a woman entered the bar, at which the barman quietly said: 'the bad language stops now'. The bad language stopped, as did the laughter, and the uninhibited chat. Two of the six pubs in the area have regular evenings of musical entertainment to which men and women both go. At these events it is not unusual for a man to spend most of his time at the bar with other men, while his wife sits with women friends, the two only coming together for the occasional dance. It is said that it looks bad for a pregnant woman to be in a pub even if she is not drinking.

Many families contain one person who is very knowledgeable about the affairs of the various family members and who keeps them all in touch with family news. Such people are referred to here as kinlinkers (compare Firth et al., 1969). Within Glengow it is far more common for a kinlinker to be female than to be male, which is not surprising considering the considerable involvement of women in familial and domestic affairs (see also Buckley, 1982). Of the seventeen out of twenty people who replied in the affirmative to a question as to whether their family contained a kinlinker or not, fifteen stated that the kinlinker in their family was a woman. [2] There was a tendency for younger women to state that the kinlinker in their family was their mother or an aunt, that is, a woman of the ascending generation; whereas older women tended to name a sister, a cousin or themselves as their family's kinlinker, that is, a woman of their own generation. The typical kinlinker thus tends to be a middle-aged or elderly woman. Adult married children who regularly visit their parents typically meet

---

[1] But see Gamarnikow (ed.) (1983), for criticisms of this viewpoint.

[2] The question asked was 'Is there somebody in your family who keeps all the members of your family in touch with family events (e.g. weddings, illness, etc.)?'

their siblings there as well as having contact with them outside of the parental home. The statistical analysis, however, provides only equivocal evidence bearing on this point, in that there is only a very small difference between sibling contacts (as measured by mean contact index) where the mother is alive as compared to when she is dead. [1]

TERMS OF ADDRESS WITHIN THE FAMILY

The strong family-orientated nature of the society and the extended period of attachment to parents may be reflected in the choice of terms used by people to address and refer to their parents. Firth (Firth et al., 1969) saw kin relation terms as indicators of appropriate social behaviour, and wrote of 'the significance of kinship terms, particularly terms of address as indices of relative status' (ibid., p.306). It is suggested here that the widespread use of terms of address and reference that are elsewhere used predominantly by children is an indication of the sustained importance that the parent has for the adult within Glengow society. (There is no reason to suggest that Glengow is significantly different from any other part of Northern Ireland in this respect, but the following discussion pertains only to Glengow and the surrounding area). In the United Kingdom 'mummy' and 'daddy' are terms commonly used by young children to address their parents. In later childhood or young adulthood other terms such as 'mother', 'ma' and 'mum' may be adopted. In parts of the United Kingdom, kin terminology is class associated; the terms 'mum' and 'dad', for instance, are in wide use among the working class while 'mummy' and 'daddy', when used by adults, are terms that tend to be limited to the upper middle class. The class structure of Northern Ireland is not equivalent to the class structure of other parts of the U.K. The use of the terms 'mummy' and 'daddy' in Northern Ireland is not limited to any kind of elite but is very widespread. Indeed, in Glengow, 'mummy' (or 'mammy' or 'mommy') and 'daddy' are overwhelmingly the most common forms of address. Virtually all women address their parents in this way, as do a large number of men. A small number of men used the terms 'mother' and 'father' while there was only one example of a woman addressing her parents in that manner and even she thought that her family must be rather formal to use such terms. Other terms in use by respondents are 'ma', 'mama', and (rarely) 'mum', and, for the father, 'da' and 'dad'. The parental terms of address commonly fall into pairs - 'mummy' and 'daddy', 'mother' and 'father', 'mum' and 'dad' and so on. However, in Glengow, as in the Firth et al. (ibid.) sample of middle class London families there are some cases of cross-pairing with the more formal female term being linked with a less formal male term, for example 'mother' and 'dad'. An explanation offerred by Firth et al. for this is that the term 'father' suggests an authority pattern to which people might be unwilling to concede much weight. Of such instances they say (ibid., p.309):

Unconsciously, perhaps, for the most part, the father was stripped of his most formal attributes, but the mother was allowed to retain hers.

---

[1] Average contact index for all siblings on the woman's side is 14.67, average contact where there is no mother 14.06 (see the previous chapter and Appendix D for details of contact index).

It may be that the role of mother is one that has not and perhaps by its very nature cannot change substantially over time, whereas the role expressed by the term 'father' is more specific and implies an authority figure that is no longer appropriate for many families today.

There was only one instance of a personal name used to address a parent, while in the Firth et al. sample a small but significant number of his respondents addressed one or other of their parents in this way. The extensive use of kinship terms in Glengow, and in particular the preference for the 'childish' terms of address, may indicate that people are very firmly positioned into their familial role, and have a stronger emotional attachment to their parents than is common in other parts of the United Kingdom. Arensberg and Kimball (1968) suggest that the prevalent use of the terms 'boy' and 'girl' to refer to people well into their adulthood is a reflection of the subordinate position that children are in vis-a-vis their parents. Although they were writing of County Clare in the 1930s these terms are still in common use in both the Republic and in Northern Ireland, and Arensberg and Kimball's point may remain valid today.

A final point on kin terminology is to make reference here to the Irish use of the word 'friend' to mean kinsman or kinswoman. This usage can lead to curious statements such as when two friends (in the English sense of the word) discovered that they were distantly related and one exclaimed in mock horror, 'You're not a friend of mine!'; or when a close friend (again in the English sense of the word) can be described as a stranger. Leyton argues cogently that this 'ambiguity of terminology' is not merely coincidence. In writing of 'Aughnaboy' he states that (1974, p. 96):

> The demands of the kinship system are such that for the majority of the adults in the village, friendship can be found only among one's 'friends'; that is, among one's close cognatic kin .... The web of constraints is such that the individual must pledge his exclusive loyalty to his kinsmen. To bring non-kin into the realm of friendship would be to weaken the solidarity of consanguines and threaten the social and economic security of all.

Even affines are viewed with some suspicion and are not conceptually regarded as one's 'friends', thus a man will speak of his 'wife's friends' when referring to his affinal relatives. The caution with which affines may be regarded is illustrated by a woman with a married son who said, 'when people marry into your family you have to be careful what you say, because you don't know what is going out'.

It is not unusual for a married woman to be referred to by her maiden name (although not addressed as such), especially if she is originally from the area. For example, a long-time married woman in her late sixties is known as Bridie Docherty although she is addressed as Mrs Connolly. In an area where a large number of people share the same name this custom serves to aid identification of the individual, but also reinforces the enduring association with the natal family. Another common usage also incorporates these two aspects, as in the case of a man whose father, Harry, had been dead many years who was still known as Harry's Dan. The kin terminology which is in common use in the area gives an indication of the central position of the family in the lives of the people of Glengow.

CONCLUSION

The type and the extent of care which takes place within the family is
likely to be at least partially determined by the nature of the family
in the society under study. Factors such as the type of family
organisation and the way in which the family as an institution is
perceived by the people of Glengow need to be considered as well as the
extent of familial contacts and the degree of affectivity within
individual families and so on. We have endeavoured to present these
aspects of the family within Glengow society as a background to the next
chapter which deals specifically with family care, particularly of the
elderly and the disabled.

4 The family and informal welfare

The family plays an important role in providing support of various kinds to its members. At one end of the scale, familial support takes the form of occasional aid-giving which presents little or no inconvenience to the donor; at the other end, however, familial support can involve a considerable degree of time, energy, and long term commitment.

TYPES OF FAMILIAL SUPPORT

Four types of familial support have been identified from our data. The four types, which do not form discrete groups as some overlap exists between them all, are categorised as follows: simple contact; advice and information giving; practical assistance; caring and tending. The first type of familial support, that of contact, refers to the contact between an individual (ego), and any members of his or her family who live outside ego's household. The other types include support which comes from within the household as well as that which comes from the family outside of the household.

Simple Contact

The basis of any form of family support is contact between family members, whether face-to-face, by telephone, or by letter. In order to examine the extent of <u>personal</u> contact between close kin, a sample of 59 households was taken - approximately one in three of our total sample. We wanted to obtain, for each of these households, an indication of: the number of close kin; the number of close kin in close residential proximity; and the number of close kin in frequent contact with the household of ego. (For the purpose of this analysis 'close kin' is defined as ego's parents and siblings, ego's spouse's parents and siblings; and any children of ego currently residing outside the household. Close contact is defined as that with kin who live within twenty miles of ego and who are in contact at least once a month). The mean average number of close kin in this sample was 9.2, and the mean average number of close kin in close contact ('close kin contact') was 6.0. That is, our respondents had, on average, six members of their close kin who lived within around twenty miles and whom they met at least once a month.

As might be expected, the frequency of contacts decreases with distance. The majority of relatives live within about twenty miles, or half an hour's drive, from Glengow, and around three in five of our sample households had cars. Effectively there is a sharp break in frequency of contact beyond five miles (that is outside the immediate district) and again at twenty miles. Of all relatives seen within a week 91 per cent lived within twenty miles.

Some instances of familial contact will offer a greater degree of affective or practical support than will others. Some meetings between family members may appear to be devoid of a supportive aspect, merely being part of the day-to-day or week-to-week routine of the individuals concerned. However, such routine contacts may provide reassurance that one is still part of a social group while their absence implies social isolation and loneliness.[1] It is noteworthy that Hunt's study (1978) found that social visiting was one of the main things desired by the elderly. Contact is most likely to be at the more supportive end of a continuum in situations which involve the elderly and the disabled. Support may often be a response to a crisis, and familial contacts that had hitherto been largely a-supportive may adapt to changed circumstances. For example, Rosie regularly visited her parents who live eight miles away, yet it was only when Rosie's husband 'battered' her, and she took her three children and went to stay with her parents, that the contact clearly became supportive. It is because familial contact is flexible and adaptive to changing circumstances that it can be so important to so many people. With the exception of the occasional family feud, family relationships tend to be enduring. It will be seen later that relationships between friends and neighbours are rarely as resilient or as flexible.

Affective support is very important within many families. Some people feel it to be virtually a betrayal of their family to take a problem to somebody outside of the home. The question 'Who would you turn to for help if you were feeling down and just wanted somebody to talk to?' prompted a large number of people to name a member of their family.[2] However, this is not the case for everybody: some people prefer to confide in a friend or an outsider,[3] while a number of people clearly

[1] 'Visiting has an important role to play in preventing or at least reducing loneliness' (Bayley et al., 1985, p.59).

[2] Two-thirds of the respondents named a member of their nuclear or extended family in reply to this question.

[3] See Mayer and Timms (1970) for some explanations as to why certain people may prefer not to turn to members of their own families for assistance.

consider confiding in anyone an unfamiliar or inappropriate form of behaviour. The following comment from a middle-aged married man illustrates this viewpoint. He had been asked as to whom he would be likely to turn if he were depressed and replied: 'I think when it comes to that, you cry alone type of thing. One should never be depressed anyway'.

Advice and information giving

The second type of familial support distinguished here may be provided primarily by one person within the family, but may involve, at different times, various family members, depending on the nature of the advice in question. Included within this group is assistance given in connection with official correspondence. For example, Eddie, an elderly bachelor farmer, always goes to his sister for help whenever he has any forms that need to be filled in. And Jack, an unemployed man in his fifties, goes to his married son for help in sorting out difficulties with his unemployment benefit. In another case, a young unmarried farmer has helped his father's sister and her husband to apply for a grant to enable them to do building work on their farm. Also included in this group is information about available work. This is commonly passed between family members.

Practical assistance

Practical assistance takes many forms; common instances are baby sitting, shopping, and odd jobs around the house and garden. Examples from our interviews are Mrs Butterley who 'perms' her mother-in-law's hair for her, and Eileen (who lives and works in Scotland) who thoroughly cleans and even paints and decorates her parents' home when she comes back on her regular visits. Eileen will also go to the house of two of her mother's bachelor brothers to tidy and clean.

There is also the example of Mrs Hammett, who cleaned and occasionally did the laundry for her husband's brother when his invalid wife was alive. An important aspect of practical assistance in many families is economic. This too can take different forms. An elderly widow with a young adopted daughter has three adult children who contribute financially at certain occasions:

> June always brings me my Christmas shopping at that time of year, and Julie always brings me Christmas shopping, so it is great. It is much better than money. At least with what money you have you can buy what you want with it. I bought her (i.e. the adopted child) a bicycle at Christmas and the aunts and uncles gave some money towards it as a present for her.

Gift giving, particularly among low income families in our sample, operates as a way in which practical goods are obtained and relationships are positively affirmed within a ritual setting. In one working-class family, Christmas presents mostly took the form of clothes which were self chosen and were being worn some days before Christmas. Gift giving constitutes a transfer of economic resources; the element of surprise which characterises gift exchange in wealthier families is absent here. The giving of land on which to build a bungalow is an example of a situation in which financial assistance is given and is not an uncommon one. Practical assistance may also arise in this situation. For example, one young married man is building a bungalow with the active assistance of his father and brother.

Most farms in the area are fairly small family farms which employ a minimum of hired labour (with the exception of potato-gathering time when a large number of hands may be taken on). Similarly the shops in the town of Glengow are small family businesses, although the bigger shops employ assistants. It is likely that just as most of those born into a farming family will have the opportunity to work on the farm so most of those born into business families will have the opportunity to work in the business. It can be seen that the family is not only important in providing information about available work, but is also, for many, the provider of work itself.

Loans and gifts of money may also be given within the family, although nowadays, depending on the situation, some people prefer the privacy of a bank loan.

Caring

This section on caring looks at the type of family support on which our attention has been mainly focused throughout the project, and deals particularly with those families in which a member is either chronically sick, disabled or elderly and frail.

The first main point to be made is that most carers, both in and out of the home, are women. This is not something that should be slipped in at the end in an appendix, but is central to our understanding of caring. The role of women as carers has been well documented in recent years (see especially Finch and Groves, 1983, Nissel and Bonnerjea, 1982, Ungerson, 1983, and E.O.C. papers 1981, 1982a, 1982b). The prominent place that women take in the field of caring arises directly from their role in the family. The last chapter discussed gender roles in the family and in Glengow society. It was suggested that the bipartite division in society whereby women come to be associated with the private domain of the home and the family, and men with the public domain and the world of work, has implications for the profile of the carer in this society. As Graham writes (1983, p.16):

Caring tends to be associated not only with women, but with those private places where intimate relations are found. Specifically caring is associated with the home and the family.

The family, however, does not exist as an isolated institution but is firmly embedded in, and has a symbiotic relationship with, the wider society. The role of the carer is concordant with the role of the woman in both the family and society (ibid., p.22):

The caring role ... is constructed through a network of social and economic relations, within both the home and the workplace in which women take responsibility for meeting the emotional and material needs not only of husbands and children, but of the elderly, the handicapped, the sick and the unhappy.

The second main point is that within the family the main burden of care commonly falls to one person rather than being shared equally among family members. That person is more likely to be a woman than a man

[1] and of the immediate, rather than the more distant family. The reasons for this arise largely from the nature of the family in this society, namely the essentially private nature of the individual family-household. And so the care of a disabled child becomes an extension of the child care tasks for which a mother (rather than a father or a cousin or a friend) in Glengow is primarily responsible. Similarly, the care of an elderly relative is far more likely to be undertaken by a woman than a man. There is a greater tendency for an unmarried daughter to take on the task of caring for an elderly parent, than for her unmarried brother to do so. So too, a married woman is more likely to care for an elderly parent than is her married brother. However, an unmarried child is more likely to care for a parent than is a married child, even if this means that an unmarried son is to be the carer rather than his (married) sister, for, as noted in the previous chapter, the family-household is highly valued and it is considered that one's initial loyalty should be to the members of one's household. An example of this situation is of a youngish unmarried man who cares for his elderly mother. His married sister helps out by occasionally sitting with her mother in the evening to enable him to get out to a bar. The tendency for a woman to 'marry out' and move to her husband's home town means that in many cases married daughters live at least a small distance from their parents. In situations in which there is no unmarried adult child or married daughter living nearby to care for an old person, the wife of a son will commonly undertake the caring role. For example, Mrs Ross, who is married with six children, cares for her husband's mother. In cases of chronically sick or disabled married men or women, their spouses normally take on the role of primary carer. However, it is noticeable that when a man is caring for his wife, more help is received from family, neighbours and friends and from the statutory social services than is the case when a woman is caring for her husband. For example, when Mr Hammett cared for his chronically sick wife for many years he received considerable practical assistance from his brother's wife.

Our third main point here is that although the main burden of care commonly falls to one person within the family, some assistance may be given by other members of the family, and where this is the case the strain upon the carer may be greatly eased. Sally Clark did most of the work involved in caring for her husband's elderly cousin but Daniel Clark did help to an extent - 'after all, she is his cousin'. Both have full time jobs. It was a joint decision for them to have his cousin Ethel to live with them: 'We both decided, it wasn't imposed on me in any way'. Sally describes her husband as having been very supportive and says that he helped when he could, for example he made breakfast for the whole family so that Sally could get Ethel washed and dressed. Very importantly for Sally her husband appreciated the work that she did in the care of his cousin:

> He was very aware of what I had to do for her, not that I would ever have said 'look what I am doing for your cousin' but he was quite conscious of how difficult it was at times.

---

[1]   Nissel and Bonnerjea (1982) estimate from their small sample of family carers of the elderly handicapped that the average time spent on a weekday on care activities was 3 hours and 11 minutes for a woman, and 13 minutes for a man.

Daniel mainly helped by doing jobs that Sally would otherwise have had to do, and by being supportive. He was not very involved in the actual care of Ethel for Sally felt that 'it did not seem to be a man's job to wash her'. However, latterly, when Ethel's health and strength deteriorated, Daniel had had to hold Ethel up while Sally washed her. The care of Ethel was also shared, to some extent, among some members of the family outside of the household. Ethel used to go to Daniel's brother and sister-in-law at weekends until they had a second baby and felt that they could no longer cope. More recently she went to Daniel's sister on a Sunday. Sally says: 'My in-laws were good about taking her; she wasn't left with us'. However, the ultimate responsibility for Ethel lay with Sally precisely because it was within her household that Ethel lived. As she said of the situation before Ethel died: 'It seems that if there is a hiccup in their life then they wouldn't take her, but if there was a hiccup in mine I was left with her anyway'.

Mrs Heneghan is a widow with nine children, all adult. Three of her sons live at home, one of whom, Jimmy, has Down's Syndrome. Her only daughter is married and lives some distance away but visits every week. Her other five sons are all married and they all live close by and visit regularly and often. One of Mrs Heneghan's daughters-in-law comes round to give Jimmy a bath every week. Two other daughters-in-law help to clean the house. Help for Mrs Heneghan with Jimmy comes from within the rest of the family rather than from her own daughter, on account of the closer residential proximity of the daughters-in-law. The care of Jimmy has always fallen mainly on the women of the family. When Mr Heneghan was alive Mrs Heneghan never asked him for help with Jimmy as he was too busy with his own work and was away from early morning to late at night: 'he was never much with the family at all'. It was Mrs Heneghan who was in charge at home and Mr Heneghan never objected to that.

It can be seen, then, that some carers receive assistance from other members of the family. However, the presence of other family members may, in some circumstances, not be a help but be a further burden for the carer. A family consisting of young children as well as a disabled member is an obvious example of such a situation; even adults may present a problem if they have demands which need to be met. Jimmy Heneghan has a quick temper and this used to be a problem for Mrs Heneghan when her husband was alive. Her daughter-in-law explains:

> She didn't know really what would be the first thing he'd have to complain about ... It used to be that she was really on edge just waiting on him coming in. Now when her husband was alive (he died three years now in July) he had a serious heart complaint, and maybe more reason then she'd have been more on edge, in case of _him_ (her husband) being upset and all as well...

Our fourth main point is that few _choose_ to take on the role of carer. In most cases, circumstances beyond the control of the individual place them in a situation in which caring is, or seems to be, the only option. There is very little choice involved in the decision as to whether or not to care for one's elderly parents, a chronically sick spouse, or a disabled child. It has been suggested that a carer, having once taken on that role, may find herself caring for one dependent relative after another, caught in what Rimmer (1983) calls the 'caring cycle'. That is, she becomes defined as a carer by her family and perhaps also by officials of the statutory services (although the term 'carer' is unlikely to be used by the members of the family). This is likely to have less to do with her actual qualities as a carer than with other factors such as her perceived availability; her probable non-involvement in a work career; her low level of training and skills; the expectations of the family and the community; and her own sense of familial responsibility. For example, Queenie, an unmarried mother of two children, lived with her parents on a small housing estate. At one point, her grandmother, who lived in an old cottage in a nearby townland, became too frail to look after herself so Queenie took her children and went to live with her grandmother and cared for her until the old lady's death. Some time after this, Queenie's mother died and the task of caring for her father, who was paralysed from a stroke, fell to Queenie; she cared for him until his death. Since then she has worked as a home help and a childminder as well as caring for her own two children. Her life has thus so far consisted largely of caring, in one form or another. The task of caring fell to Queenie rather than to her sister, who is married with just one child. As a married woman her sister's first loyalty was expected to be to her husband and child, whereas the loyalty of the unmarried Queenie was still expected to be to her natal family. Despite having two children, Queenie had not formed her own family-household which entails marriage and a separate residence.[1] As a single parent Queenie had little freedom of choice regarding housing and work, her maternal commitments tied her to the home and rendered her 'available' for further caring work.

CONCLUSION

Care giving within the family (as opposed to general familial exchange of information, goods and services) is not an haphazard event but is bound by recognized, yet unstated, rules as to who cares for whom, and how. Very little choice is involved for the carer as to whether or not to take on such a role. The rules of care within the family arise directly from the structure of the family, and the value accorded to family life. Such values are held within the family and within the community, as well as shaping a number of policies within the statutory provision of social services and benefits.

------

[1] Queenie is commonly addressed and referred to by her Christian name, whereas she addresses and refers to most women by their title, i.e. with the prefix Mrs. This is an indication of her anomalous position (i.e. she is a mother yet she is not a wife), she thus cannot be addressed as either 'Mrs' or 'Miss'.

5 Neighbourliness and neighbourly care

This chapter examines neighbourly aid and the conditions on which it is given. References are made in particular to the aid given to the disabled and elderly. Our discussion of the giving of aid and care is first located within the context of a wider examination of the values shared by people concerning their neighbourhood.

PERCEPTIONS OF THE NEIGHBOURHOOD

It is necessary to have some appreciation of the way in which neighbours and neighbouring are viewed in Glengow in order to understand the nature and extent of that care which is given by neighbours. There exists in Glengow, as in many places, an ideology of neighbourliness. The replies given to questions about neighbours are invariably along the lines of 'I've got very good neighbours indeed, couldn't have better' and 'the neighbours are very, very good'. The people of Glengow are very keen that their town should be seen as a friendly place. An elderly lady spoke of Glengow in this way:

> Every one is very friendly and anyone round this way would do anything for the other, that sort of way. There is no one who would see you in want or trouble or that sort of thing if they could help you out.

People from the Glengow area view their home place very favourably in comparison with big cities which are considered to be unfriendly and where, it is believed, most people do not even know their next-door neighbour. The peacefulness of the area is also frequently stressed and contrasted both with urban life in general, and with those areas, urban and rural, of Northern Ireland that are badly affected by 'the troubles'. An elderly man expressed himself in this way:

I can't understand all these troubles we have in Northern Ireland at the present time. I can't see why people can't live in peace and harmony without all this trouble ... The people in Glengow all live together. It does not matter what your religion is, there is nobody who would interfere with you. With regards to religion, you go to your church and I go to mine and that's that, that's all there is to it.

There is a tendency to deny the presence of sectarian conflict in Glengow, but although some residents might assert that the area is trouble free (and it is true that there are few violent incidents) it has the reputation locally (for Catholics at least) of being a 'bitter' place. Furthermore many of the Protestants from the town and from the eastern lowlands consider Ballyreagh, in the south-west, and to a lesser extent Killyullin, in the north-west, to be full of I.R.A. sympathisers and consequently a potentially troublesome area.

More important, however, in terms of our interest in informal welfare, is the view held by the people of Glengow of it as being a caring place. This is mainly expressed in terms of the rural nature of the area. A middle-aged man from the town said:

I think old people in big cities are worse off than people here in the small villages of this country. They are probably more associated with their friends or with their family or something like that. I have been in cities in England and I have seen old people, and how they managed I never understood ... I suppose it happens here in cities as well, but not so much in a rural district. People live different.

Another comment, this time from a middle-aged woman who lives just outside the town, was that 'country people are not inclined to have their elderly parents put into an old people's home'.

The concept of Glengow as a caring community is largely expressed in terms of the care afforded by the family, and, to a lesser extent, by the 'friendliness' of neighbours and the apparent willingness of neighbours to help when needed, particularly in a crisis.

However, Glengow is considered to have been more friendly in the past than it is today. It is commonly said that whereas in past years there was a great deal of ceilidhing, especially in the rural area, today little or none takes place. There are a number of commonly held explanations given for its decline or demise; here an elderly Protestant man speaks of how things were:

It used to be around this district you would have gone to this house tonight and some other house tomorrow night. We had a house for nearly every night, but that is all done away with. With television and all the rest of it people have other pastimes apart from the visiting, they do not visit the same at all and they have motor cars now so they just step into the car and go some other place, before that, when you just had the bicycle or something like that, you just had not the same pastimes as they have now.

An elderly Catholic woman spoke in a similar vein about ceilidhing and its decline; however, her two unmarried brothers still do ceilidh and she indicates why:

A man had a certain house to go to every night or maybe the same house for two or three nights, and they would sit and talk and maybe play cards or something like that, but now the television is on and most people have television in their own house. Mickey and Kevin don't because they don't have the electricity and it's the people who don't have the television who would still go on a ceilidh or a visit ... Mickey would come here the odd time and he goes to my sisters and to places like that - cousins' houses, places like that.

It appears that ceilidhing takes place largely among kin rather than among neighbours in general. The following remarks from a middle-aged Catholic woman also indicate this: 'unless you were going to someone's house with a message or it was your own friends and relations or something like that, you would not dream of going to visit in a house'.

Nowadays ceilidhing is an activity that is not only largely conducted among kin but specifically among those kin who live near one another. There is not a great deal of contact between non-kin neighbours. The woman to whom we just referred has her own opinion as to why there is much less contact with neighbours than there had been in the past:

I will tell you what I discovered about neighbours since I came here. When I came here I drove a car and you would never get to know your neighbour when you get into your own house in your car and you go about your business in it... When I was a youngster at home you walked everywhere, and we came out to church on a Sunday and there they were, coming in droves down the road, and we all came down and we chatted and we yarned and all the rest of it and you got to know everybody, all those people that we met, and you heard of all their aches and pains and all that type of thing ... Now you get into your car and you go out, you don't really have the same contact when you are not out walking as we used to long ago.

Glengow has grown over the last twenty or thirty years with new housing estates being built and people from the surrounding countryside moving into the town itself. Some of the long-time Glengow residents now comment on the fact that they no longer 'know everybody in Glengow'. One shopkeeper born and reared in the town estimates that he now knows only half of the people in Glengow today. A number of people who have moved into Glengow from outside of the area are related to Glengow residents. Some newly-married couples from Glengow might accept housing elsewhere only to return to Glengow as soon as housing became available there. It can be difficult for new non-kin residents to get to know other people purely as neighbours. Social contact tends to arise through common membership of certain associations, for example, the church, the local Orange Lodge, or the Women's Institute. Even those associations and organisations which are not avowedly religious or political in nature tend to have a membership which is limited to one or other of the two main religious groups.

Newcomers to the town do not always share the view advanced by the local people concerning the general friendliness of the place. George has lived in Glengow for ten years. He does not consider Glengow to be particularly friendly although he has made some friends in the town and considers that he has good neighbours. He says:

Glengow ... is a very insular place. You can get some people who will speak every time you meet them and others who will only speak when they want something. Again you will get a few who will speak one day and not speak the next day, for no apparent reason.

Although he gets on well with both sets of next door neighbours, the neighbours on one side are particularly good to him. His comment here about them illustrates the helpful but unintrusive role that a good neighbour is expected to play: 'I would find these here extremely helpful. They are very friendly, very friendly, but not overpowering. If they feel you don't want them, that's it, they'll go'. Other neighbours, however, would 'only help just to find out what's happening'.

George was widowed eighteen months ago. At the time of his wife's death many people rallied round to help:

> I couldn't have asked for better neighbours at that time or better friends anywhere ... People rallied round, even people that I barely knew helped out which I found surprising. Like Betty, for instance; just dropped everything and helped, and in her case it didn't stop after a few weeks like most things do - you have a death in the family and everybody rallies round and helps out and then it gradually tapers off - in her case it didn't. She started inviting us down for tea once a week and then that's carried on now. And again, there are others you think, looking back in retrospect, funny that they didn't offer any help or that they didn't come round.

Neighbours will help out in a crisis and are expected to do so. But the point that it can be difficult, especially for newcomers, to establish regular social contact with neighbours is borne out by the case of the Whittakers. Mr and Mrs Whittaker have lived in Glengow for four years and they are not very happy there as they feel rather isolated and friendless. Their own kin, with whom they have little contact, live some distance away. Mr Whittaker describes the people of Glengow as follows: 'People can be distant, they can be very friendly at the same time very distant. It's a strange mixture'. Mrs Whittaker went on to say that 'here they appear to be very smiley and friendly and you feel that you've made a friend and - you haven't really'.

If newcomers do not consider Glengow to be a friendly place it is largely due to the fact that they are less involved than the indigenous population in local networks of aid. This is because most networks of aid are kin based. The ideology of Glengow as being a 'friendly' place blurs the distinction between kin and neighbours, partly because in a number of cases kin and neighbours are one and the same thing, and partly because somebody who is considered to be a 'good' person will be good to his family and good to his neighbours, although different meanings are attached to the two types of acts of 'goodness'.

The amount of social contact between non-kin neighbours who are long-time residents of Glengow is not large, although there is, of course, considerable variation between different people and different households. For example, a woman was heard to remark that she rarely sees her neighbours and that she had not seen her next-door neighbour for over two weeks. People may be described as good neighbours even if rarely seen. C. and M. Ball (1982) distinguish between four different layers of neighbourly involvement. The first level is where neighbours are seen every day or every few days and although no contact or communication takes place (for example, a neighbour may be regularly seen from a window by somebody who is housebound) some picture of the neighbourhood is built up. The second level is the level of talk and communication; the exchange of greetings at least. The third level involves the exchange of goods and services. At this level an equality of reciprocity may be important. The fourth level is that of dedicated involvement in the life of a neighbour. Applying these ideas loosely to Glengow it can be seen that the first and second levels may be virtually all the 'neighbourliness' that some people experience. However, this is sufficient to enable many of them to view the area as 'very neighbourly'. Many people's involvement with their neighbours is, however, of the third level. There is very little evidence of the fourth level of 'dedicated involvement'. In general it seems that a good neighbour in Glengow is someone who does not intrude into another's life but is there if needed. 'If the neighbours could do you a good turn then they would do it', is a comment whose sentiment was expressed by a number of people. It suggests the rather backstage role that a good neighbour is expected to play. The notion that neighbours are waiting for an opportunity or invitation to be helpful rather than constantly offering help arises partly from the fear of being viewed as interfering and is an indication of the 'Ulster modesty' about which Harris (1972), among others, has written. To go too far out of one's way to help others might be construed as immodest, as implicitly boasting about one's own good fortune and position. It is also the case that each of those interviewed and asked to comment about neighbours is a neighbour, thus to suggest that neighbours would help out if needed enables such people to see themselves as good neighbours without necessarily ever having been actively involved at all with neighbours.

Some Glengow people believe that the older areas of Glengow are the most friendly while others feel that there is more contact between neighbours on the new estates (for a discussion of the 'myth' of neighbourliness, see Buckley, 1983). In many respects the High Street is different from the other areas. Its residents tend to be older, of higher social status and more likely to be in possession of a car and a telephone (valuable means of facilitating communication). Their relatives are more widely dispersed than those of respondents from the housing estates. This suggests a pattern of greater geographical mobility which is borne out by the fact that the median number of years that these respondents had lived in their present house is relatively low – five years (compared with a median of ten years for respondents living in the housing estates). Differences not only exist between the High Street area and the housing estates but also between the various housing estates. For example, Treetop Park, the oldest of the housing estates, which was built in 1950 is well established and neat and prosperous looking. The residents are predominantly skilled manual workers (class 3 in the classification explained in chapter 2) and middle-aged with few young children. This estate pre-dated the setting up of the Housing Executive and it appears that its earlier residents were selected on rather different criteria than those in use today. A former member of the Rural District Council then responsible for housing in the area said that they had tried to allocate the houses in Treetop to 'decent people'. In contrast, Hollyberry Drive and Silverbirch (built in in the mid-seventies and 1967 respectively) have a younger and more transitory population than Treetop. Nearly half of the households sampled in these two areas contained at least one child under the age of eleven. However, too much weight should not, perhaps, be laid on the relatively small differences between the housing estates, even though a variety of experiences of neighbouring is indicated by them, for the main difference in the town lies between the estates and the owner-occupied High Street area. The differences here suggest a considerable variation in the texture of neighbourhood life which is likely to be reflected in the nature and extent of neighbouring. For example, in Silverbirch there are a number of young women, several of them with small children, who are constantly in and out of each other's houses, borrowing and lending small items, sharing cups of tea and sometimes the care of each other's children. In contrast, a respondent from the High Street who has lived there for over ten years said that she had no contact with neighbours. She did, however, have several middle class friends scattered throughout the town and its surroundings, some of whom shared in her recreational activities. While the physical lay-out of the various areas should not be ignored, these two extremes may be taken as illustrating Allan's (1979) distinction between working class 'situational' and middle class 'constructed' friendship.

In order to elicit further information on aid-giving two questions (15a and 15b) in the PPRU survey of Glengow town asked to whom the respondent would turn for help if he or she was ill and needed shopping done, and to whom he or she would talk if feeling 'down'. Approximately two-thirds of the respondents said that they would turn to kin and a third to neighbours in these two situations (compare with Wenger, 1984, p.125). It appears that people in the newer, less stable areas have a relatively higher degree of non-kin contact than people in the older, more stable areas. This is in accordance with the findings of Buckley (1983) yet is not in line with the findings of some other writers, for example, Abrams (1977) and Stacey (1975). The relatives of rural respondents were much less dispersed than the relatives of those in the town. This helps to create a close-knit community, for <u>the categories of kin and neighbour overlap</u>.

In general, Glengow people feel that the past was more friendly than the present, and that rural people are more friendly than urban. This last point both contrasts Glengow with the big cities of the Province and of England, as well as presenting a contrast between rural Glengow and Glengow town. Perhaps it is not surprising then that there exists a considerable variation in the nature and degree of neighbourliness in the Glengow area.

NEIGHBOURLINESS

Variations in the social contact and aid-giving that take place between neighbours may be due to a number of factors including:

(i)   proximity of residence;

(ii)   duration of residence at a particular address and within Glengow;

(iii)   length of time of acquaintance;

(iv)   common workplace or work experience;

(v)   common church membership;

(vi)   common life-cycle situation (variations over time may correspond to the life-cycle of the individual. For example a mother with young children may have considerable contact with women living nearby who are in a similar situation, yet contact may not continue once the children reach school age or once they have left home);

(vii)   family ties or connections (where known kin are near neighbours there may be social contact and mutual exchange of aid, not because they are kin _per se_ but because as known kin they are known to each other);

(viii)   the availability and readiness of one neighbour to offer aid to another (someone who is greatly involved with his neighbours in terms of social contact and aid-giving is likely to have few or no close kin or to have little involvement with his kin);

(ix)   personal likes and dislikes.

The forms of aid exchanged between neighbours cover a wide range of goods and services. However, the aid is not generally of an intensive and long-term nature, for such aid giving is more characteristic of care within the family. The goods and services commonly exchanged amongst neighbours fall into four main groups: the use and loan of commodities; visiting and social contact; lift giving; and general services.

The giving or loaning of certain commodities are fairly common occurrences among many neighbours. Home-produced vegetables are given and exchanged, small domestic items are borrowed, and an item such as a washing machine or a telephone may be used by neighbours.

Visiting and social contact between neighbours vary in frequency and depth of interaction. Events occur at which neighbours meet and socialise although the professed reason for these is not primarily in order to facilitate neighbourly contact. For example, wakes, funerals and weddings serve to bring neighbours together and may be attended by near and distant neighbours. Events such as 'gift' parties tend to be limited to nearer neighbours. Most contact between neighbours occurs informally; it is not uncommon for one household in an area to act as the focal point for neighbourly interaction. For example, the house of Elsie, a middle-aged woman with three children, is frequented by many of the local children as well as their mothers, and has become a meeting place for neighbours who rarely, if ever, go into each other's houses.

The example of Mr Baldwin is instructive in many ways. He is an elderly man in his eighties who suffers from varicose ulcers and therefore finds it difficult to get about, although he is not housebound. He lives on a small housing estate in a publicly-owned bungalow which is designated for old people. Mr Baldwin has a home help, Mrs Kennedy, who lives nearby, and he is also visited regularly by some of his neighbours. Mr Williamson is a middle-aged married man who is a near neighbour. He calls on Mr Baldwin every evening to see if he needs anything. Mrs Campbell lives next door to Mr Baldwin with her husband and children and her husband's mother, and she calls on Mr Baldwin to see if he needs any shopping done. Other neighbours also visit; Mrs Kennedy occasionally visits in the evening and watches television with him as does another neighbour. Other people from the town visit him as well as friends from further afield. Mr Baldwin himself visits his neighbours who are housebound. He goes next door to visit the older Mrs Campbell who is ninety years old and very frail. He also recently spent a lot of time with an elderly near neighbour to try and cheer him up as he had become ill and depressed. Mr Baldwin has lived in Glengow all his life and at his present address for over ten years. He is the first cousin once removed of his elderly neighbour, Mrs Campbell. There is also a family connection between Mr Baldwin and his home help as Mrs Kennedy had previously been married to a cousin of his. When Mrs Kennedy spends time with Mr Baldwin beyond the hours for which she is paid it is not clear whether this is primarily to do with her role as a state paid home help, as a neighbour, or as an affinal relative of Mr Baldwin. It was noted earlier that it is not always possible to distinguish between ties of kinship and ties of neighbourhood and Mr Baldwin's situation is illustrative in this matter.

The giving of lifts is a very important service for people living in a small town such as Glengow, situated as it is in a rural area. Many of the examples of lift-giving from our data are casual arrangements, although a number of cases involve the regular provision of a lift by one neighbour for another. In some cases a further service is incorporated with the lift-giving. Every week, John Grant, an unmarried man in his thirties who lives with his parents, drives his elderly next-door neighbour, Mrs Smith, three miles into Glengow in order that she may collect her pension and do some shopping. He not only gives Mrs Smith the lift but also helps her with her shopping. Mrs Smith explains:

> Well as soon as he comes home and gets his dinner he takes me to Glengow every Thursday for my shopping and my pension ... he comes into the shop with me and carries out my basket and everything; you would think I was his mother.

Three points arise from this example. Firstly, Mrs Smith has known the Grant family all her life and they have been next door neighbours for over forty years; this fits in with a suggestion that the longer the period of acquaintance the greater the tendency for neighbourly contact and aid to be established. Secondly, John Grant works part-time and has told Mrs Smith that if he found full-time work he would be unable to continue this service. This is an indication of the constraints on neighbourly care, the availability of neighbours to help in terms of their own work, family, and other commitments. Thirdly, the service which John Grant does for Mrs Smith is described by her in familial terms: 'you would think I was his mother'. Her comment expresses the commonly held belief in the primary role of the family in the care of its members.

Another example of lift-giving is provided by Mr Salisbury, a retired man in his sixties, who regularly gives his neighbour, Mrs Docherty, a lift into town. Both Mr Salisbury and Mrs Docherty have been widowed. They live a couple of miles outside of Glengow and go in daily to do their shopping. They have been near neighbours for forty years and the families have always got on very well although they are of different religion. Mr Salisbury was at pains to stress that there are no sectarian tensions among his neighbours:

If the neighbours could do you a good turn they would do it. We are all on good terms and no ill-will or ill-feeling, it does not matter what your religion is, it is all the same. The Dochertys there and me were always very great and even when Mrs Docherty's father-in-law and mother-in-law were living we were very friendly and they came in here and we went over there. Religion did not matter at all.

Mr Salisbury and Mrs Docherty are involved in an exchange of services of which lift-giving is only a part. An illustration of this is given here in Mr Salisbury's account of what good neighbours the Dochertys are:

These people over the road here, they are great neighbours. After the wife died Siobhan said to me (that's the girl who teaches) 'some day we will go to Farreaghly and I will get wallpaper and I will paper your room for you' and I says 'That's all right, whatever you say'. And I went down with them and we got the wallpaper and I bought a new carpet and Siobhan came over here and she done all the paintwork and she papered the walls and she made a real good job of it. That is the type of people they are. They are real good neighbours, very good to me.

For all the lengthy time of their acquaintance and the aid that has been exchanged over the years Mr Salisbury still refers to and addresses his neighbour as Mrs Docherty, and she refers to and addresses him as Mr Salisbury. The relationship is not an intimate one, and this is typical of relations between neighbours. Boundaries are maintained between neighbours, one expression of which is the use of formal terms of address. A good neighbour is not someone who intrudes into one's life; a good neighbour does not become 'one of the family'. A good neighbour is someone who is friendly and helpful and available when required.

Although people may extend to their neighbours aid of various kinds and of varying degrees, the greater part of care of the elderly and the handicapped which takes place 'within the community' actually takes place within the family. There is reluctance among carers to ask neighbours for assistance in the care of their dependant. Part of the reluctance stems from the feeling that the responsibility of care is too great to place upon a neighbour. Many carers claim that if they asked for help then they would receive it, but they prefer not to ask and would prefer people to offer. The widow of two sons described as 'backward' says:

If I needed help from my neighbours then I would get it, although people don't really offer. I don't very often ask, to tell you the truth, unless it's something I just can't handle on my own.

The mother of a handicapped boy remarked that 'nobody ever offers, I don't like to ask'. And a woman caring for an elderly relative made the point that in the case of a critical illness or of death there is no difficulty in getting people to help but it is far more difficult to get help with everyday problems that require a long-term commitment. She said: 'I would never expect people to help on a long term basis for the sake of neighbourliness'.

There are, of course, exceptions. Mrs O'Hagan cared for her elderly next door neighbour for three years 'just out of neighbourliness' and expressed the hope that someone would do the same for her when she gets old. This voluntary caring arrangement was transformed into a formal paid arrangement when Mrs O'Hagan learnt about the Attendance Allowance and the home help service.

CONCLUSION

The following points summarise our main findings about neighbouring and caring.

1 Neighbourliness in Glengow is primarily latent rather than active, that is, it operates mainly at the Balls' (1982) first and second levels. The countervailing virtue of privacy is often implicit, if not explicit, in people's attitudes and practice.

2 Neighbouring appears to be stronger in the rural area of Glengow than in the town itself, especially in a closeknit and relatively homogeneous area such as Ballyreagh.

3 Neighbouring is also relatively strong among poorer and younger respondents. There are class differences in neighbouring as Allan (1979) and others have argued.

4 There is evidence to suggest, perhaps surprisingly, that neighbouring may be quite strong in the less settled neighbourhoods (housing estates). However, it is worth pointing out that in reply to the question (in the PPRU survey) regarding to whom the respondent would not turn for help, the only category of person which was mentioned with any frequency was that of 'newcomers to the area or people you don't know very well'. (See Appendix B for Question 16 on PPRU questionnaire). But it is worth noting that this reply came more often from the longer-established areas.

5 It is apparent that in some circumstances neighbouring is likely to occur between neighbours simply because they have known each other for a long time.

6 Popular ideology has it that neighbouring has declined over the years. Greater prosperity, increased urbanisation, and changes in farming methods that reduce the degree of co-operation needed between farmers (see Bell, 1979) suggest that this is indeed the case.

7 Neighbours tend to play a subsidiary role in the care of the disabled and elderly, with the great bulk of the care falling to the family. However, in those cases where neighbours provide social support for the disabled and old, and also for the principal carer, this is greatly valued.

8 Neighbours may play a more important role than usual in the care of the elderly and disabled in situations where caring relatives are absent (see chapters 9, 10, and 11, and Hunt, 1978).

6 Coping with care

As we have seen, most caring takes place within the family home. That being so, our discussion now refers mainly to care within the family rather than to care by and for neighbours. The occasional exception to this does, however, occur, and it is made clear in the text when such an instance arises. We begin with a section which explores the kind of contact that carers have with statutory welfare agencies, and their views about it. Part of the section is devoted to our findings about the perceptions of both carers and non-carers of the responsibilities of social workers. The next section reports on the main problems directly associated with caring – including isolation, financial hardship, anxiety about the future, and the difficulties of the actual caring task themselves borne by carers. The final main section discusses, by contrast, some of the satisfactions of caring.

DEALING WITH THE STATE

The very fact of having an elderly or handicapped person within the household may bring people into contact with the state in a way which might not otherwise happen. However, despite such contact, the amount of information held by some people about the available services and benefits was found to be far from complete. Information about benefits was not always acquired from professionals working for statutory agencies but was passed on through informal channels. For example, Sally Clark, who cared for the elderly senile cousin of her husband, learnt of the Attendance Allowance (for which she was eligible) through two non-statutory sources – an old school friend and St. Vincent de Paul. Another example is of Bridie Hegarty, the mother of a profoundly disabled child, who learnt of the Attendance Allowance and the Mobility Allowance through her sister's friend who also had a disabled child.

This woman also told Bridie about the Joseph Rowntree Memorial Trust Fund. Bridie applied and received money which enabled her to purchase a washing machine and a tumble-dryer - two items of great benefit to Bridie. This is not the only case we came across of a parent of a disabled child passing information on to a parent in a similar situation. However, Bridie then mentioned a near neighbour who had had a disabled child, who had died, and who knew about the Trust but had 'never bothered' to tell Bridie about it. Another respondent, to whom we have already made reference, only learnt through informal channels that she might be entitled to financial recompense from the state for her labour. She subsequently was employed as a home help and also received the Attendance Allowance.

Social workers have a low profile in Glengow, largely because there is no social work office in the town. Several problems which in Farreaghly would be referred to and dealt with by social workers are, in Glengow, dealt with by those 'professionals' who are on the spot, namely the police and the general practitioners. For example, it was Sally Clark's G.P. who arranged for her husband's cousin Ethel to be admitted to hospital for two weeks in order that Sally and her family could take a two-week holiday. Sally says that her doctor was aware of her situation and was always helpful and asked how she was coping. Sally regularly saw the doctor throughout this period as she was pregnant and was attending the local clinic. The frequent contact between Sally and the doctor served to remind him regularly of the burden of care under which she laboured. Mrs Leyton, the mother of a Down's Syndrome child, was told about a group for parents of Down's Syndrome children by the consultant whom she saw in connection with her daughter. It was from attending this group that Mrs Leyton first heard about the Joseph Rowntree Memorial Trust Fund.

Sally considered that all the doctors with whom she had had any contact over Ethel had been very helpful. For some weeks prior to Ethel being admitted to a geriatric unit two nurses helped Sally with her at home. She says that these nurses were helpful too, although initially they 'came in on the defensive and had to be convinced of the need of them being there'. Sally felt that they had misconceptions about her. She felt that they thought that because she was a lawyer she would be 'too nice' to clear up after Ethel.

In general, little interest was expressed in having contact with social workers. When Sally applied for the Attendance Allowance she was asked on the form to indicate by whom she would like to be visited. Sally ticked 'social worker' although she did not particularly want to be visited by anybody. A social worker came to visit when Sally was out and left a card so that Sally could get in touch, but she never bothered to do so. Bridie Hegarty's attitude to social workers is that she is 'not interested in social workers coming round to my house unless there is a special reason. If I want something I know that they are there'. This is not because Bridie has had a negative experience with social workers; on the contrary, she appreciates the efforts of the social worker who arranged for her to receive special items for the bath, and a push-chair. In the case of Mrs Milligan difficulties arose when she did want contact with her social worker: 'you ring up to speak to a social worker that you have seen and are told that they are on an in-service training course, or have been promoted, or have left'. She is unhappy about the high turnover of staff among social workers. She feels that the situation was better in the past when you just had one social worker who got to know the family well and stayed for years.

We wanted to assess the degree of knowledge held by our respondents about the role of social workers and of some of the statutory social services. To this end we included questions in the PPRU interviews designed to elicit such information. Half of the respondents in these interviews (that is, fifty people) were asked the question: 'What do you consider the main tasks of social workers to be?'. Sixty-one answers were given because some people offered more than one answer and we chose to record them all. Twelve people (that is, 24% of the respondents) gave a 'don't know' reply. Of the remaining replies, while none of them were 'wrong', some were very vague and rather idealistic. For example, three replies said (in varying words) that social workers should 'show a kindly face to people', and three spoke of community spirit and the need to get the community together. The biggest group of answers (42.6%) was to do with the care of the elderly, the handicapped and the very young. Nine answers (14.8%) were to do with poverty and people in need. Only one answer expressed reservations about the duties of social workers by saying that they 'shouldn't take children away from their mothers or put old people in homes when they don't want to go', although another comment was that social workers should be more energetic in keeping an eye on cases of child abuse.

The remaining fifty respondents were asked to comment on two 'vignettes', each of which describe a social problem.[1] These were presented in the following manner:

I am going to read out two examples of people who are in difficulty, and I would like your opinion.

a. Imagine you know a family where the father has been off work for some time and living on sick pay. They are having trouble making the money go round and are getting behind with the electricity. Where do you think they should go for help?

b. Suppose an old couple live next door to you and for a few months you have been getting worried about them. Their home is badly in need of decoration and their health is failing. You know that they are too independent to ask for help and yet they seem to need it. Who do you think should help them?

Sixty replies were given for the first vignette. Five of these were 'don't know'. A large number of replies (37) suggested that the family should contact social services or social security (it was not clear from the answers on this questionnaire as to what extent, if any, our respondents distinguished between social services and social security. For this reason we group these together). Only three answers suggested that relatives or friends be turned to for help (as noted elsewhere it is difficult in Ireland to distinguish between these two terms). Eight replies suggested going to the Electricity Board. The type of person traditionally seen to be in the role of advice giver was hardly mentioned. Thus although one person suggested the priest, and another suggested getting in touch with the politician Ian Paisley ('he'll sort them out quickly'), there was no mention of a doctor, a schoolteacher or of a councillor.

---

[1] As mentioned in chapter 2, these are derived from the work of Glastonbury et al. (1973) and Glampson et al., (1977).

The second vignette received sixty-five replies, four of these were 'don't know'. The combined figure for answers suggesting that the social services and social security should help was twenty-one. Relatives and friends were suggested in eighteen replies and neighbours in fourteen. Two replies suggested the priest or minister, and three the doctor. As with the first vignette there was no mention of the local councillor.

The first vignette presented a problem which was primarily financial. The replies received suggest that there is a low expectation of financial help from relatives. There seems to be no expectation of financial help from neighbours, as there was no mention of it at all. Instead, there were many replies suggesting that official bodies such as the 'welfare' and the Electricity Board should be contacted. In contrast, the social problem presented in the second vignette was seen to be one that could and should be dealt with by relatives or by neighbours. There was a larger number of replies than there had been to the first vignette, which suggested that the 'traditional' advice givers should be contacted. A number of replies indicated that the family and/or neighbours should be the first to help out, and only if they were unable to do so should the 'welfare' step in. Some replies suggested a combination of informal and formal types of support. For example, one respondent said: 'I should (help them) for a start, and also would advise their doctor, and recommend them to make their situation known to social security and possibly their minister'. Questions about the knowledge held by people about statutory benefits and services deserve more attention than they have so far received. It would be particularly useful to compare groups of people with different needs: the elderly; the handicapped; carers of the elderly; carers of the handicapped; parents of young children, and so on (but see Glastonbury et al., 1973; Glampson et al., 1977; and OUTSET, 1982).

DEALING WITH THE PROBLEMS OF CARING

The problems faced by the carers in our sample fall into three main categories which are as follows:

isolation, boredom and a restricted life

financial hardship and worry about the future

problems intrinsic to the actual tasks of caring.

Not every carer is affected by each of these problem areas. Some carers may be affected more by one concern than another, or may be affected at different stages throughout the timespan of caring by one problem rather than another. For many carers there are satisfactions as well as difficulties involved in the tasks which they undertake, and these too may change over time. This section and the next endeavour to present both the problems and the satisfactions of caring as they have been presented to us by carers in Glengow. In as many cases as possible we let the statements of the carers speak for themselves.

Isolation, boredom and restricted life

The life of a carer may be considerably restricted by the tasks and commitments of their role. Some carers are very conscious of the narrowness of their lives, while others appear to have adapted or resigned themselves to it. An example of a carer who is very aware of the extent to which her life is limited by her caring role is an elderly woman who cares for her arthritic husband. She is a cheerful, sociable woman who would like to be able to get out of the house and meet people. However, she says: 'I suppose while we are both spared I have to stay in with him. No, I don't get out too much, it gets very monotonous in the house for me'.

She would have liked to have joined the Women's Institute, but 'he doesn't like me away from him, so I belong to nothing'. She gets out to church occasionally, depending on the condition of her husband. It is apparent from her statement that when she does manage to go, a certain amount of organisation is necessary; spontaneous outings are rarely possible for carers:

> I don't get out every week, but through the summer I got to church every Sunday, for I set him here after I dressed him and he stayed in this chair until I got back. I was not out last Sunday, for I would not leave him, and I will hardly get out again until he is out of bed again.

Mrs Flynn is a widow who lives with her three teenage sons, two of whom she describes as 'backward' and attend the local special care school. They live on a farm in the hills outside Glengow. All the work of the farm and the family falls to her since the death of her husband four years ago, and she finds it a great strain. The son who is not attending special care school is unemployed but offers little help to his mother. Mrs Flynn feels lonely and isolated especially since her husband died. This is not simply due to the loss of her husband himself, but also to the loss of regular visitors, some of whom came by every night when her husband was alive. These days she just gets the 'occasional odd straggler', and says that 'people don't have as much time for you nowadays'. She herself rarely goes out visiting. When the boys were younger she could not depend on any one else to watch them, she knew them inside out whereas others did not. However, she recalled: 'many a time I would have liked to have gone out'. Nowadays she hardly goes out as she would not do so alone, and although she would go out with one of her daughters she rarely does because 'they are busy with families of their own'. She considers her life to be very boring and quiet: 'if it gets any quieter it will stop'.

An example of the extent to which the care of a disabled relative may restrict the carer's own life is that of the mother of a physically disabled girl who attends the local school (see chapter 8 for more details of this case). When the girl first attended the school it was arranged that a special assistant would be available in the school to attend to her needs. After a short period of time the special assistant left the school and was not replaced 'because of the cuts', so the girl's mother goes to the school four times a day, to take her and collect her and to administer to her needs during the break and lunchtime. She consequently could have had little time available in which to do her general housework, apart from any other activities.

A carer may have little available time for social interaction with friends and with neighbours, or even with those members of her family outside of the household or the immediate vicinity. As noted earlier, outings of all kinds can involve a great deal of organisation and preparation. Lack of ordinary social contact may result in the isolation of the carer. Where there is little every day social contact it may be very difficult for a carer to ask neighbours or distant family for help with his or her charge. There is a strong tendency to attempt to contain problems within the immediate family; members of the family who live outside the household (i.e. who are married and have families of their own) are assumed to be busy with their own immediate family and are not expected to contribute very much. As the mother of a Down's Syndrome boy said: 'he is my responsibility; every woman has to look after her own'. While carers may be loathe to ask for help, the wish that their family and neighbours would <u>offer</u> to help was expressed by many of them. The mother of an eight year old handicapped boy told us:

> I don't like to ask, no. Unless people would offer. Now my father <u>occasionally</u> if he was at home or there was something <u>particularly</u> we wanted to go to ... I remember once when I was awfully upset and I really wanted to go out this night and he (her father) wouldn't say yes and he wouldn't say no. I just stamped out of the house and he followed me up the road and I was sitting in the car crying, and he had no patience and he said 'Would you quit your crying', and I said 'I never ask you, but if you could just say yes or you could just say no, and I never ask you to babysit or do anything for me'. 'Of course I'll babysit, of course' and then he is the best. He took them all down and gave them their tea. But he would not think of offering.

In times of crisis the family and neighbours rally round to help out, but the uneventful day-to-day tasks of caring remain largely within the immediate household and commonly fall to just one person.

Financial hardship, and worry about the future

Financial hardship is experienced by a number of the 'caring families' from our sample. It is not always easy to isolate the prime cause of hardship. In particular, it is not possible to pinpoint the presence of a disabled family member as being the sole or main cause. But the presence of an elderly or handicapped dependant in the family is very unlikely to improve the financial position of a household. In the cases of families on a low income any worsening of their financial situation may be critical.

One of the main causes of poverty in the United Kingdom is unemployment. The unemployment rate in Glengow is 24 per cent, which is average for Northern Ireland and is considerably higher than the overall rate for the United Kingdom. Wages in Northern Ireland are lower than in the rest of the U.K. but the cost of living is higher. The economic position of a family can usually be expected to fluctuate throughout its lifespan. Hardship is experienced by a number of families when their children are young, eases as the children grow up and leave home or contribute financially to the household, and returns as the stage of retirement is reached. In families in which a male breadwinner is in full time employment <u>and</u> which do not include young children little financial hardship may exist even if a family member is an elderly or disabled dependant. Nevertheless, where a family is dependent on state benefits or a low income the presence of a disabled family member may be a considerable drain on limited resources.

However, neither the fact that certain people are in full employment whereas others are not, nor that of those in full employment certain people get promoted and others do not, are purely matters of chance. Leaving aside the contentious issues of class, educational opportunities, race, and religion, and focusing solely on that which has specific relevance to carers of the elderly and the disabled, it can be seen that financial inequalities may arise between families of able-bodied members and those families which contain one or more members who are disabled and dependent. Lesley Rimmer (1983) examines the cost of care by looking both at the additional expenses which 'caring families' may incur, and at the loss of income from earnings when a carer is forced to give up work or reduce hours of work or forego promotion opportunities because of the commitments of the caring role (see also Baldwin, 1985).

Along with personal poverty may be added a difficult environment, especially for those living in rural areas. Some of the worst aspects of rural deprivation have been alleviated over the years although the lack of a good public transport system remains a problem, particularly for low-income families. Mrs Flynn, the mother of two subnormal boys, describes her life as having been very difficult when the children were young, for in those days their farmhouse had no water and no bathroom. Mrs Flynn had to walk half a mile to fetch water from the well. Ten years ago water was brought up from the river and at this time a bathroom was put in. Just three years ago water from the main public supply was provided. Of those early days Mrs Flynn says: 'We managed, it was a struggle but'. Today, the Flynn household is still struggling, for with two sons at special care school, one son who is unemployed and Mrs Flynn now widowed, there is little money available. The farmhouse is in a poor state of repair and an air of depression pervades the place.

Mr and Mrs Brown have five children between the ages of ten and eighteen living at home; the youngest of these is a boy with Down's Syndrome. Mr Brown is a retired farmer and Mrs Brown does not work outside of the home. When the children were younger Mrs Brown found it more difficult to cope than she does now and she applied for a home help but the application was turned down. Nowadays things are easier because the other children are there to help - she never asks the neighbours to help and her own family live too far away to help out although they would do so if asked: 'we just manage within the house'. They have never had a holiday. Mrs Brown would like to go away on holiday but they cannot afford to do so.

Money can be used to buy a variety of commodities that help to make life easier, including practical assistance. When the Browns' application for a home help was turned down they were not in a financial position to pay for help. In contrast, Mr and Mrs Clark, a professional couple, who had Mr Clark's elderly cousin Ethel living with them, could afford to pay for a housekeeper by using Ethel's money for just that purpose:

> Ethel wasn't a financial drag in any sense, she had her pension and the Attendance Allowance, we could afford to pay for help - her money paid for the housekeeper.

Mrs Clark was not prepared to give up her work in order to look after
the old lady. However, she and her husband were committed to caring for
her and wanted her to live with them rather than in an old people's
home. She says: 'relatives are ones own responsibility, one shouldn't
for convenience dispose of them into institutions'.

Many carers worry about what will happen to their charge in the
future. Carers of disabled children are concerned about what their
children will do when they leave school at sixteen, and about who will
care for the children when they, the parents, become too old and frail
to cope or when they die. These worries may be slightly offset by the
hope of some carers that their child will become increasingly able to
cope with certain aspects of everyday life. This will vary with the
ability of each child; carers of profoundly handicapped children are
unlikely to hold on to such a hope. Others may be disappointed; the
mother of a sixteen year old subnormal boy said that three or four years
ago her son Willy used to be quite helpful, but that now he has no
interest or energy and she does not know why: 'it is so disappointing,
I thought that as Willy got older he'd get better'. The main worry for
the carers of disabled children in our sample concerns leaving school.
Mrs Flynn said: 'I think they will have to leave the special care
school at sometime, and that's when the worry will start'. Mrs
Milligan, the mother of a handicapped boy, expressed the worry of many
parents when she said: 'What happens to them after sixteen, that's the
big problem; where do they go after sixteen?' She continued:

> They all end up in day centres like Farreaghly Day Centre with all
> kinds of old people and very handicapped people, and that is where
> they go at seventeen years of age, and as someone said 'I do not
> want my child sitting in a wheelchair all day listening to music and
> twiddling his thumbs'.

Mrs Milligan and her husband had frequently discussed the problem of
their son's future:

> He is nine now and I will battle from now to get something. I
> suppose like every other parent you hope that there will be
> something better when he is sixteen. This is what gets my husband
> going so much, the thought of what happens to him. He says if we
> had land, if he were a farmer, if we had money ... he always says
> about money, but I don't think money makes anybody happy. He says
> that if you had something to cushion him with, if you had a business
> or something that he could go into and be protected, you could
> protect him. He thinks that money would protect him in someway or
> another. I don't know that it would do.

For the carers of elderly dependants the concern is that the elderly
person may become increasingly frail and in need of more care and that
the carer's own health and ability to cope will deteriorate over the
same period of time.

Problems intrinsic to the actual tasks of caring

The actual problems associated with the tasks of caring vary from case
to case and consist of practical problems as well as less tangible
issues. The type of problem will vary with such factors as: the nature
of the handicap; the financial situation of the family; and the extent
of support received from other family members, neighbours, the voluntary
and statutory social services, and the private market in welfare.

<u>Problems of constant care</u>. The need of some disabled people for constant care and attention can result in a carer being restricted to the home and becoming very isolated; this was considered earlier. Here, carers speak about how they experience the actual demands of constant, or nearly constant, care.

Mrs Milligan says of her nine year old epileptic son Seamus, aged nine:

> At home I could say he is an absolute pest, he has everybody tormented and it is non-stop 'do this, do, do, do' it is 'me, me, me, me' ... it is 'play with me, do this with me', that's non-stop with him ... he demands attention all the time.

Yet a carer cannot watch literally <u>all</u> the time and so problems arise. The mother of two sons of subnormal intelligence described one as being 'beyond watching'. He got her into trouble with her neighbours for a while as he had the habit of letting livestock out. Seamus Milligan did a lot of damage to their house and broke various possessions such as a stereo, a television, and a window that cost over a hundred pounds to replace:

> Any room I would put him in, there would be something in it for him to wreck. All our doors are bashed in. If you look at the house — the calamities that have happened.

Other situations involve charges who are helpless and need to have everything done for them. The problems of constant or nearly constant care are partly alleviated for those carers whose charges regularly attend an institution of an appropriate kind, either on a daily basis as the majority of the handicapped children in our sample do, or on a weekly basis as, for example, Seamus Milligan does.

A number of carers mentioned that they rarely or never got a full night's sleep due to the demands of their caring role. Bridie Hegarty's profoundly handicapped five year old son spent the first year of his life in hospital, since then neither Bridie nor her husband has had one uninterrupted night's sleep in four years. Mrs Jones whose handicapped son died at the age of eight said: 'I reckon he slept a month of full nights in his life'. When Mrs Heneghan's Down's Syndrome son was young she spent eighteen hours a day with him constantly, and during the remaining hours between midnight and six in the morning she would have been up and down a few times attending to him.

<u>Practical Problems</u>. The sheer physical weight and strength of the person being cared for can present problems. Mrs Cox cared for her mother up until the time of her death. Her mother was a big woman and when she fell, as she occasionally did, Mrs Cox was not capable of lifting her alone and if her husband was not available she used to ask the man next door for assistance. Similarly, Mrs Milligan has difficulty in lifting her son Seamus these days: 'I can't lift him now because he has got so big and heavy, and when he is in a tantrum and he is kicking and flinging I just can't lift him now'.

Conversely Sally Clark found the practical task of washing Ethel's hair a problem once Ethel became so weak that she needed to be physically supported: 'I didn't really know how to do it, I don't know how they manage it in hospital'.

Incontinence can be a particular difficulty. Carers of somebody who is incontinent find that the amount of laundry that needs to be done can be enormous. So much so that Sally felt that the main difference made to her life when Ethel went into hospital for a short stay was that there was less washing to be done.

Effect of caring on family life. The twin difficulties of finding people who express a willingness to sit with a disabled person and the reticence of many carers to ask, means that a carer may rarely go out on normal family outings. For example, a married woman carer may find that she and her husband rarely spend an evening out together. Sally Clark and her husband very rarely went out together when Ethel was living with them because of the problem of getting somebody to sit with her. Mrs Milligan would occasionally like to go out to some event at the weekend, but as Seamus returns from school to them every weekend she cannot do so. However, Bridie Hegarty, the mother of a profoundly handicapped boy, says that she 'gets out plenty'. She comes from a large family and one of her sisters and her mother have looked after John on different occasions. Not everyone is willing or capable of looking after him. For example, John sometimes needs to have his nose pinched while being fed and one of Bridie's sisters feels that she would not be able to do that. But the fourteen year old daughter of Bridie's next-door neighbour 'works with him great' and Bridie is happy to leave John with her if she wants to go out on a Friday or Saturday night. Yet Bridie would not trust anyone to look after him for a weekend or longer.

A carer in a family in which there are (other) children may worry about the effect on them of her caring for the disabled family member. Sally Clark did not feel that her four children suffered by the presence of Ethel in the home and the amount of time required from Sally to care for her, yet she says:

> I didn't feel any deep sense that the children were deprived, yet I would have Ethel washed and dressed in the morning before Sarah (her four year old daughter). I was more careful with washing and dressing her than with my own family.

And Mrs Milligan recalls when Seamus wrecked the family holiday and the other children were upset. Here she recounts one incident out of many:

> He just wrecked the holiday ... One day on the beach I remember. I was out in the garden doing something and I could hear him squealing, and the next thing the second boy came back and just sat in the corner. He couldn't speak, he just couldn't speak. 'He is at it', he said, 'he picked a row and had a tantrum and everybody is looking at him'. He had walked home embarrassed and disgusted ... I came back and I said never again. I said I would never go on holiday with him again.

Difficulties in the relationship between the carer and the cared-for. It is normally expected that members of a family care about one another, and where a member needs to be cared for it is assumed that the 'caring for' (i.e the tasks of tending), go hand in hand with the 'caring about'. Although this is not always the case it is very difficult to elicit information about feelings of antipathy within a family, and 'caring families' are no exception to this (see Briggs and Oliver, 1985). Even where much affection exists between a carer and a cared-for, there may be occasional or frequent difficulties in the relationship.

In many cases of caring a relationship between the carer and cared-for will already have been established prior to the 'caring' relationship as such - for instance in those cases of somebody caring for an elderly parent or for a spouse who has become handicapped through an accident or illness. In cases of caring for a parent there may be feelings of love and affection and a sense of obligation to repay past affection and care. However, people may find themselves caring for a parent for whom they feel little or no affection. Equally difficult are situations where the carer did not actually know the cared-for prior to the onset of caring. Sally Clark, who cared for her husband's elderly cousin, was in this position, and recalls: 'I had no relationship with her because by the time she came here she was incapable of forming a relationship, she was doting'. At times the old lady behaved unpleasantly to Sally: 'I remember once when I was lifting her feet on to a cushion and she kicked me on the chin. That was quite normal, it was so hurtful'.

Sally says that if the task of looking after Ethel were to be presented to her now she would do the same thing again and take Ethel into her home and care for her, but she would have considerable reservations: 'I think I would die a death if I had to do it again. I would hate to live my life over again. I found it _extremely_ difficult'.

The relationship between a carer and a disabled child may also present occasional difficulties, even when there is mutual love and affection. Jimmy Heneghan's quick temper and Mrs Heneghan's consequent anxiety has already been referred to.

SATISFACTIONS OF CARING

Despite the many problems and difficulties associated with the care of the frail elderly and the handicapped, there may also be some satisfaction to be derived from it for the carer. In many cases it seems that the problems and satisfactions of care are intertwined. Sally Clark recalls one time when she was doing something for Ethel and Ethel said to her 'thank you darling, you're a good girl'. Sally felt like hugging her yet points out that this was the only expression of gratitude she received from Ethel in three years. As already noted, Sally and Daniel Clark are strongly in favour of caring for one's elderly within the family, and they would have derived satisfaction from the knowledge that they had cared for Ethel through the last years of her life up until her death. However, this was denied to them since Ethel died in hospital where she was staying temporarily while Sally went into hospital herself to have her fourth child. They were very disappointed that she had died in hospital:

We wanted to bring her home to die. I would have had her home on the day I came home from hospital if I had thought that she was going to die there ... We had endured so much for so long, it was like tripping at the end of the race after you've run a mile.

Other carers too referred explicitly to some of the satisfactions of their caring role. Mrs Milligan, having spoken at length of the difficulties and frustrations involved in the care of her son, ended up by saying: 'there _are_ the good times, it is not all bad times'. While Mrs Heneghan, speaking of how ill her Down's Syndrome son had been when young, and of all the hours of constant care that she has given him through the years, said: 'I had a hard time rearing him, but it was worth it all, he's come out of it rightly'.

CONCLUSION

The care of an elderly and/or disabled person may involve care from three different sources, namely, the family, neighbours and friends, and the statutory services. We have already argued that care for the elderly and disabled falls mainly to members of the family, and commonly to one woman within the family (see especially chapter 4). The rather limited nature of neighbourly care in this connection has already been indicated. Here we want to conclude by stressing some points about the predicaments and needs of carers as seen by the carers themselves.

Relatives are largely cared for within the family because, as Sally Clark said: 'relatives are one's own responsibility'. In Sally's case this was still considered to be so even although she, the main carer, had virtually no relationship with the elderly relative by marriage for whom she was caring. The feeling that 'relatives are one's own responsibility' is especially pronounced when the person in need of care is a parent, spouse, or child. Having taken on the caring role, the carer would like to achieve a sense of worth and satisfaction from the task, in order to make personal sense of all the difficulties and deprivations. It is understandable that Sally was disappointed that Ethel died in hospital after having cared for her at home for a number of years ('we had endured so much for so long'); and that this feeling of disappointment could co-exist with her having found the task of caring very difficult - 'I think I would die a death if I had to do it again'.

Isolation appears to be an ever-present part of the life of many carers. The essentially home-based activities of caring places them in a similar position to that of the housebound mother with young children. While much has been written on the isolation of mothers within the home (see Gavron, 1966; and Oakley, 1974), less attention has been paid to carers, many of whom are in a comparable or worse position. Bayley, in his work on the mentally handicapped and their families, writes (1973, p.183):

> Almost all the families were subject to the sort of restrictions which are associated with a pre-school child ... this state of affairs had not been a matter of a few years, just a stage through which the family passes, but had persisted for the subnormal's lifetime, and the ages of those visited ranged from sixteen to seventy-one.

Carers may become socially isolated as well as being physically isolated within the home. Many then find it difficult to ask for help and expressed the wish that family and neighbours would offer aid. Social and affective support, if not forthcoming from the family, tended to come from those in a similar situation to themselves.

One of the differences between care within the family and care by a neighbour is that the neighbour can, in general, choose whether or not to care; as one woman said of her elderly neighbour: 'I took pity on her'. This is not, of course, to deny that pity or compassion is felt within the family towards their disabled or elderly members.

The attitude of carers towards the statutory social services and benefits tended to be fairly critical, although this may be because criticism in general is more readily expressed than praise or satisfaction. Thus the benefits and aid received from the statutory services were not usually singled out for acclaim, whereas negative experiences were mentioned. The high turnover of staff in the social work office has already been mentioned as being particularly distressing for one woman. The perceived attitudes of some of the 'caring professionals' occasionally came in for criticism, although others, in particular doctors, came in for some praise. Sally Clark's comments about the nurses who came to help her with her elderly cousin, and in particular her feeling that they thought that she would be 'too nice' to clear up after Ethel, raises interesting points about how women who work in a 'non-caring' job outside the home are viewed. It is unlikely that a nurse, health visitor or home help would have been considered to be 'too nice' to clear up after an elderly incontinent relative.

'There are the good times, it is not all bad times', says Mrs Milligan the mother of Seamus. This chapter has endeavoured to identify those factors which contribute to the bad times, and those which facilitate the good times. The following factors are those which contribute to the well being of carers and consequently, the cared for. Each factor will, of course, vary in its relevance and importance for different people in different situations.

1 Access to information about benefits and services.

2 Helpful professionals, whether doctors or nurses or social workers. Continuity of contact with these people is felt to be important. But carers want help from the statutory services on their own terms. They want support at the time at which they ask for it, and they do not want to be patronised.

3 Support from the family and from neighbours. Practical support from kin and neighbours is often welcome especially if it is offered; there is frequently a reluctance to ask for help. However, support can also take the form of emotional support. One carer specifically mentioned that having the support of her husband made her task of caring easier.

4 Financial security.

5 A sense of security about the future. For example, the uncertainty felt by a number of the parents of disabled children about their child's future, in terms of the availability of places in special care schools and sheltered workshops, was a constant source of anxiety.

6 A sense that the best was being done for their charge.

7 Access to transport.

8 Free time away from their charge.

In general terms it is possible to say that these factors are positively correlated with the feeling of carers that they are coping adequately and are reasonably happy in their role of carer.

7 Disabled children and their families

The four previous chapters have been concerned in relatively general terms with the informal aid and care that flows between kin and neighbours in Glengow. This chapter considers our findings which relate to one of the specific groups within Glengow on which we have been focusing, namely disabled children.

There are nine households in the Glengow area in which there is a disabled child. Seven of the ten children attend the local special care school which is at Farreaghly. They are: a mentally and physically disabled boy of four; a Down's Syndrome girl of six; a profoundly disabled boy of five; two mentally subnormal brothers aged sixteen and nineteen; a mentally and physically disabled boy of fifteen; and a Down's Syndrome girl of ten. There is also a nine year old epileptic boy who boards at another special care school during the week; a physically disabled girl of thirteen who attends the local secondary school; and a deaf boy of four who attends the deaf unit at Bankside. Of these nine households, three are presented here first as case studies to illustrate different aspects of the lives of families of disabled children. We will look in turn at the experiences of the Gresham family, the Milligan family and the Lloyd family. The chapter ends with a discussion of the main findings, taking all nine families into account.

THREE CASE STUDIES

The Gresham Family

The Gresham family are not from Glengow; they moved there four years ago from the city fifty miles away. All of their near kin live within the general vicinity of the city. The parents of both Mr and Mrs Gresham are dead. Mrs Gresham has two brothers and two sisters, and Mr Gresham has two sisters and a brother. The Greshams do not see the members of their families very often. Whereas the Greshams' siblings rarely visit them, the Greshams will try to visit their siblings on their occasional trips to the city.

The Greshams have three children. Julie, their youngest child, has Down's Syndrome. When the Greshams first moved to Glengow various people occasionally offered to look after Julie. However, the Greshams rarely took anybody up on their offer. Mrs Gresham says that this was really her fault since she has always been wary of having 'just anybody' looking after the children. She needs to know the person well first. The Greshams say, as other parents of disabled children have also said, that they understand their child in a way that another person might not. Mr Gresham says of caring for Julie that 'you need to read her', and Mrs Gresham says:

> I always like to know that a person really understands Julie. Apart from that her main problem is danger, she doesn't understand danger ... and you need to be alert when she is with you...You see, she is quite big and she's good at some things and some folk would maybe go 'oh Julie, Julie understands'. But Julie doesn't understand.

There are just two or three neighbours with whom they are happy to leave Julie on occasion. Partly for this reason the Greshams rarely go out together socially. However, they go away for a family holiday together every year and greatly value that. In general the Greshams feel isolated and are not very happy in Glengow. They say that they 'never see anyone'.

Julie attends the special care school in Farreaghly where she is happy and is getting on well. Initially, the Greshams had not wished Julie to go to the school because they did not want her to just be taken off their hands for a few hours a day and be kept amused. However, they are very happy with the school now and say that it has greatly improved since the appointment of a new headmistress two years ago. They feel that the teachers there are not just keeping the children amused but are working towards an end:

> ...all the teachers ...are now more working together, they have a vision for the children... And even if the child doesn't achieve it in the end at least they have the vision and they are giving them the opportunity. And this was all we fought for; that she would be given the opportunity. If she never reads or writes then that's all right, but we wanted to feel that she was given the opportunity, if there is any ability there then it would be brought out.

One thing which they particularly appreciate about the school (other parents have also remarked favourably upon this) is that when their child does something special at school it is written down in a note to the parents which is sent home with the child that evening:

> If there's a special achievement, or if she's maybe tackled her dinner in a particularly good manner or something, we'll get a note home saying Julie did something today. It's great, you know, because she can't come in and tell you, her speech isn't very well developed yet...there's contact between school and home all the time.

Mr and Mrs Gresham are closely involved with the school and are active in the Parent Teacher Association. Their contact with other parents of Down's Syndrome children is largely through the school. They are also in some contact with the local Down's Syndrome parents group. However, its meetings are held on a night that makes it difficult for Mr Gresham to attend, and Mrs Gresham does not drive. They attend when they can, but they feel that they 'fit' more into the school and so are more actively involved with it than with the parents group.

The Milligans

The Milligans have four children including an epileptic son of nine, Seamus. He attends a special school some miles away as a boarder throughout the week, returning home for weekends and holidays. The Milligans have lived in Glengow for little longer than the Greshams. The father and two brothers of Mrs Milligan live nearby in Glengow. Mr Milligan's family live further afield; his mother in Galway and his four brothers scattered throughout Ireland and Britain. They see very little of their kin to the point where Mrs Milligan says: 'We wonder if there is something wrong with us'. According to Mrs Milligan, her husband feels 'an awful lack of support' from his family. The two of them blame Mr Milligan's mother for 'carrying stories to the rest of the family. She has painted a black picture of Seamus'. Mrs Milligan is reluctant to ask either kin or neighbours for help with Seamus but wishes that people would offer to help. She does not even like to ask her father for help although he lives nearby. However, a cousin of Mrs Milligan has looked after Seamus on two occasions and consequently offered to have him again 'anytime'. This cousin, who lives in Belfast, used to have a disabled child of her own who died. Yet Mrs Milligan has not taken her cousin up on her offer to look after Seamus. The distance is a problem and she does not like to impose upon her.

The daughter of a neighbour of the Milligans had been very good at looking after Seamus. However, she has moved away from the area now in order to go to college. On one occasion the girl's mother offered to help even though she is in poor health. Recalling this occasion, Mrs Milligan said:

> She offered to babysit and I showed her how to use the oxygen ... and I'm sure she was in nerves 'till we came back, but she didn't say so and I always appreciate that. But those are rare people, very rare people.

Mrs Milligan says that she rarely sees the priest; he does not come in to visit on a regular basis and may not even be aware that Seamus is away at school. She would like to see more of him, but says that if she needed him he would come in to see her. She would not like to impose upon him by asking.

Three years ago the Milligans were visited and interviewed in order for their eligibility for Attendance Allowance to be assessed. This was a very distressing experience for Mrs Milligan, she described the interviewer as 'dreadful, absolutely terrible', and said that the interview had been the 'biggest humiliating experience', leaving her in tears afterwards. The interviewer insisted that Seamus remain in the room throughout the interview. He sat and listened to all that was said about him, then, after the interviewer left, 'he really set to...he had sat and listened to her and the things he had done...after she left he damaged the boys' bedroom door. The things he done after she left'. The interviewer was impatient with Mrs Milligan and objected to her using any technical terms to describe Seamus' condition, even contradicting her on occasion. For example, in response to the description by Mrs Milligan of Seamus' behaviour, the interviewer said that it was impossible for him to have all the symptoms and behaviour which Mrs Milligan claimed. Mrs. Milligan felt that the interviewer 'was tying me in all sorts of knots... at one stage I just dried up when I could not answer and I don't know whether she got the message or not. I just could not answer the way she was asking'.

Mrs Milligan found the interview so upsetting that her attitude to receiving the allowance was affected. She felt that she would rather do without the allowance than have that interviewer in the house again. Mrs Milligan particularly resented some of the questions which were asked:

> These stupid people! If you could just see Seamus when he was having a tantrum and just come and live with him and see what we are having to live with, or you went down to the toilet and he made a mess of himself in the toilet, and he is screaming at you because he does not want to be cleaned up. I would just think, just come and see how we earn your Attendance Allowance.

Fortunately the next time that there had to be an interview about the allowance the interviewer was a very pleasant man. Mrs Milligan feels that many people are not aware of their eligibility for certain allowances and thinks that this would not be the case if people were in touch with one social worker who knew their case well. She says that it used to be that you would have a social worker who knew the family well and who stayed for years, but now social workers are younger and there is a greater turnover of staff, and when you ring up to ask to speak to your social worker you are told that he or she is on an in-service training course or has left.

Mrs Milligan is on the committee of the Bush Toy Library which provides toys mainly for disabled children. In 1978 they received a small grant from the DHSS(NI) to set it up, since then financial support has come from voluntary sources, for example from Children in Need. Mrs Milligan used to take the toys to the Gateway Club in Glengow once a fortnight but found that there was a poor response to this with only two or three families attending regularly. Consequently, these days she only does home visits. She says that there is a lot of apathy among many people who have disabled children. She feels that there are people who, although they have cars and drive off to play bingo, do not bother to go to the toy library and yet would take the toys if she took them to their houses.

The Lamonts

The Lamonts have three children: their youngest is a physically disabled daughter of thirteen who is restricted to a wheelchair. In contrast to the other two families Mr and Mrs Lamont are local to Glengow and are in frequent contact with the members of their two families. The parents of both Mr and Mrs Lamont live in Glengow and are seen most days. In addition, five of Mrs Lamont's six sisters live within about ten miles, and two of these actually live in Glengow. With the exception of the sixth sister who lives thirty miles away and is seen about every six months the sisters are seen on average once a fortnight. Mr Lamont's three brothers live in Glengow and are seen most days.

Jeanette attends the secondary school in Glengow for four days a week (she has two half-days off). According to Mrs Lamont, it is largely due to the new headmaster, who was appointed at the time that Jeanette was due to change schools, that it became possible for Jeanette to go to the secondary school. Mrs Lamont says that the new headmaster is 'a man with new ideas', while 'the old master was different in his attitudes'. Ramps have been built at the school to accommodate Jeanette in her wheelchair, and there is some talk of disabled children from other towns coming out to Glengow to attend the school.

When Jeanette first attended the school she was given a teacher of mathematics and English, and a special assistant. Both the teacher and the special assistant have since left and have not been replaced 'because of the cutbacks'. In place of the special assistant Mrs Lamont goes to the school four times a day: she takes Jeanette in and is there at breaktime, returns at lunchtime and picks her up in the evening. This arrangement began on the understanding that if Mrs Lamont went in at these times (i.e. replacing the special assistant) then Jeanette would be provided with a teacher from half-past nine to half-past eleven. However, despite requests from the headmaster for the departed teacher to be replaced this has not happened and so Mrs Lamont continues to spend a large part of each day at the school with her daughter.

The Lamonts have been provided with a lift in their house to raise and lower Jeanette between the ground floor and the first floor, as well as a lift to lower her into and raise her out of the bath. Jeanette receives the Mobility Allowance. Up until a year ago she received the night time Attendance Allowance but this was then withdrawn although Mrs Lamont says that she has more work with Jeanette at night now than when she was younger. The doctor appealed against the decision but was not successful in getting the allowance re-allocated.

ISSUES ARISING FROM THE INTERVIEWS

We now try to identify and discuss the main issues which arose from the interviews with the nine families.

Kin

The amount and type of aid expected or received from kin, outside of the household, was found to vary from family to family but did not generally amount to very much. Grandparents of a disabled child were commonly too elderly to be able to offer much assistance. The siblings of the parents of the child were likely to be fully occupied with the rearing of their own families. Other children in the family are generally expected to help out to an extent when old enough to do so for as long as they remain within the household. However, once they leave to marry and set up homes of their own it appears that little assistance is then expected of them. The bulk of caring takes place within the household. The onus of the burden of care thus tends to fall largely on the shoulders of the parents, and, in particular, the mother. The amount of stress felt by the parents of a disabled child varies with the life-cycle position of the household. Greater stress appears to be felt when the disabled child is young, especially if there are other young children in the family; this, of course, can be a difficult period financially for many families. (For a discussion of poverty and families with handicapped children see Townsend, 1979, Ch. 21). When the children are older and are able to help with the disabled child or with household chores then the stress may ease slightly, only to return when the other children leave home and the ageing parents are left to cope on their own.

Neighbours

The most noticeable aspect of the relations between the parents of disabled children and their neighbours is the strong degree of reluctance felt by the parents to ask for even trivial assistance. The parents of the disabled children were very reluctant, in most cases, to leave their child to be looked after by a neighbour - either because the care of the child was considered to entail too much responsibility for a neighbour, or because it was felt that a neighbour could not know and understand the child in the way that his or her parents would. While parents were reluctant to ask for help from their neighbours they did appreciate such offers even although they might never actually accept the aid offered.

Access to Information

In some cases, information about, for example, eligibility for certain benefits or about a parents support group, came through official channels. In other cases, information came through chance encounters with parents in the same situation. For example, a woman with a disabled son learnt of the Joseph Rowntree Memorial Trust Fund (see Bradshaw, 1980) from a friend of her sister; this friend also had a disabled child. Learning about the Trust Fund proved very useful to her. She applied and received money from it for a washing-machine and a tumble-dryer - items which are invaluable in the care of a profoundly disabled incontinent child. While there was a number of examples of advice or assistance given to parents of a disabled child by someone who had a disabled child themselves, or had had one in the past, it did not appear that parents of a disabled child inevitably felt a sense of identification or solidarity with other such parents. The various social barriers in existence in the community, such as class and religion to which we referred in chapter two, did not automatically dissolve for these families.

Education

All the parents of children who were attending Farreaghly special care school were very satisfied with it. However, a number of parents had initially been hesitant about sending their child there, which appears to have been partly due to an understandable reluctance to embark their child upon a disabled 'career' (see Goffman, 1968(a)). The hesitation may also have been part of the general reluctance felt by parents towards the care of their child by virtually anyone other than themselves.

Some distrust of the motives of those responsible for special education was expressed. For example, a woman whose son had attended a unit (for children with educational difficulties) for three months was suspicious of the motives of an assessment made by the educational psychologist which resulted in her son being withdrawn from the unit. The educational psychologist said that her son had not made adequate progress there. However, the child's mother felt that this assessment was made as part of some current educational policy and that, in fact, her son's place in the unit was required for another child.

Natural Community Leaders

By natural community leaders we mean those Glengow people who are in a position of some prominence or influence in the area. They are not necessarily elected representatives of the people. These leaders appear to play a rather limited, but on occasions useful, role in assisting carers. The clergy do not offer a great deal of support, for various reasons, but the support which they are able to give is clearly welcomed. It is apparent from Mrs Lamont's account above that at least a couple of people who are in a position of some authority, namely the doctor and the headmaster, have attempted to intercede on her behalf in her dealings with the state.

Social Services

The fact of having a disabled child brought these families into contact with the state and with the social services; for at least some of them it seemed that little contact might otherwise have taken place. The parents interviewed had willingly received the benefits to which they were entitled and would accept further benefits if such were forthcoming. One woman said: 'If I was entitled to it I'd accept it'. Benefits were gratefully received while at the same time considered to be their rightful due, thus the interviewer who came to assess eligibility for the Attendance Allowance and who made a mother feel humiliated was later strongly criticised by her.

Some parents received what they wanted from social services and required no further contact except on their own terms. One woman put it like this: 'I am not interested in social workers coming round to my house unless there is a special reason. If I want something I know that they are there'. However, other parents appeared to experience a sense of powerlessness vis-a-vis the statutory social services. Reasons for this have been suggested already: it is felt that different social workers come and go, and allowances are cut with no explanation. These parents appear as passive recipients of state aid, they neither have, nor expect to have, control over their situation.

8 Disability and old age: 1

The previous chapter dealt with the rather special situation of disabled children. This and the next two chapters deal with the disabled who are adults; and also with the elderly (who for the purpose of this analysis are defined as those 60 years old and over), since a considerable proportion of the elderly are, in fact, disabled.

Before going on to an analysis of these two overlapping groups we present two vignettes to give the flavour of the real-life situations which later discussion amplifies. Inasmuch as the two cases illustrate the principles to be deduced later we shall need to return to them.

Mary Barker, single and in her late 40s, cared for her 76 year old widowed mother. Mrs Barker suffered from multiple disabilities, of which arthritis, an ulcer, and heart disease were the most serious. Just able to get about the room at the time of the first interview, she later became completely bed-ridden, and had to be fed, bathed (though a district nurse came twice a week she did not help in this) and given the bedpan by Mary, who was confined to the house except when a neighbour's presence enabled her to shop for half an hour. Mary had a 50 year old unmarried brother in the house, but he was at work during the day. Mary herself had worked in a factory in a town some twelve miles away until her mother's first heart attack, when she came home to look after her.

The family lived in a Housing Executive house in a small, long-established estate. The neighbours - two of whom were, in fact, relatives (cousins) - were helpful but could effectively only supplement Mary's tending. There were no other children besides Mary and her brother. Mrs Barker had two sisters and two brothers. One brother lived only two houses away but she was on bad terms with him, the other, living in Springdale, was slightly mentally retarded. One of the sisters, 'Aunt Millie', herself a widow, lived in Glengow, but the support she could offer was for some months reduced by her own illness. The other sister was permanently hospitalised. Mrs Barker had worked as a farm labourer and as a domestic servant in her youth. She had come from Glengow originally and had lived in her present house for a good many years.

In general this family were poor, their effective network can be described as medium and they received only basic statutory help (nursing care and financial assistance). The burden on the carer was extremely heavy, and, arguably, the situation of the person cared for was less than optimal. In fact, the burden was lifted during the course of the research: Mrs Barker died. Despite the almost intolerable nature of Mary's burden she appeared to shoulder it willingly, nor did she seem to regard it as anything but normal to give up her job to care for her mother.

The second case is that of Mrs Thompson, a lady of 80, who at the time the research commenced was living with her son and his family in a Housing Executive house in another, rather more middle/upper working class estate in Glengow (Treetop). Mrs Thompson suffered from asthma, bronchitis and heart disease, and she too died before the research was completed. Although unable to get out of the house and requiring help with feeding, bathing and toileting she was not bedfast. Mr Thompson, an extrovert, sociable man in his late 40s was an engineering tradesman in a large local factory. One of his daughters was married and at the time of the research lived next door, another was in tertiary education in England, and a third was a nurse. A teenage son commenced an apprenticeship as a mechanic during the research. The younger Mrs Thompson had worked for a time as a shop assistant.

Mr Thompson had three siblings and his wife seven. Of the total of ten, eight lived within 20 miles and two were in England. Quite close contact was maintained with the various brothers and sisters. In addition, the Thompsons, who had lived 23 years on the estate, were in frequent contact with several of their neighbours and had a considerable circle of friends elsewhere in Glengow as well as further afield. Mr Thompson's involvement in various organisations served to increase the social and geographical range of his acquaintances. In terms of occupation, social contacts and life style the Thompsons may be classified as borderline working class/ middle class: although Mr Thompson had a (skilled) manual occupation the family appeared to have a substantial economic base.

Most of the burden of care fell on the younger Mrs Thompson but substantial help, such as bathing and toileting, was offered by one of the daughters (the nurse), and the married daughter had had the old lady in her house for two years before she became ill enough to require constant attention. The clear impression given was that the family were able to cope satisfactorily with her without major detriment to their family and social life.

Although both carers were tending elderly women with not very dissimilar levels of disability, these two cases in most other respects contrasted strongly with each other and the overall situation of carers as well as cared-for was strikingly different. The implications of these findings form part of the argument of the rest of this chapter.

We now turn to a general analysis of the situation of the disabled and elderly. One may note first that it is primarily these two client groups which form the principal targets of community care (see Walker (ed.), 1982, chs. 1, 5 and 9; and Walker and Townsend (eds.), 1981, for useful recent analyses) and who - together with mothers of small children, who are also relatively immobile - are those whose situation constitutes the major argument for the 'patch' system (see Hadley and McGrath, 1980 and 1984), 'community social work' (Barclay Report, 1982) and the numerous ventures in statutory/voluntary/informal sector co-operation, exemplified in the Crossroads and similar schemes (see DHSS, 1984; Walker and Qureshi, 1983; Challis and Davies, 1980; and Parker, 1985). Apart from this clear policy relevance the causes, context, processes and 'efficiency' of informal caring by relatives, friends and neighbours are well exemplified in relation to the elderly and the disabled.

The questions explored here relate to three levels of analysis and intervention, the community (or 'macro'), the neighbourhood (or 'mezzo') and the individual ('micro') (Timms, 1983, pp. 409-13). The first concerns the material resources (statutory or non-statutory) available at the community level (and above) as well as the individual's integration into the community, in terms of participation in its social institutions, such as churches or voluntary agencies, and his/her psychological identification with the community. The neighbourhood level involves social networks, whether the extended web of kinship or contacts with neighbours and friends. The micro-level embraces the sphere of close relationships, normally within the household, and the physical and psychological resources of the person cared for and his/her immediate carer. All three levels are relevant to the needs of the individual but in different ways and in differing degrees; there is, of course, interaction between the levels. Most social policy analysis, in relation to the elderly and the disabled as well as that of social psychology and of interpretive sociology, focuses primarily on the third level. Social psychological concepts such as 'stress' (Selye, 1976; Eckenrode and Gore, 1981), 'coping' (Pearlin and Schooler, 1978) and 'crisis' (Parad (ed.), 1965 and Brown and Harris, 1978) relate essentially to the micro-level. Network concepts, it has been argued (Mitchell, 1969), provide a bridge between macro-analysis and micro-analysis. The present study, while acknowledging the utility of micro-level concepts and to some degree drawing on these, endeavours to focus on the inter-relationships between the three levels, more particularly between the situation of the individual/family and the networks in which he/it are embedded.

There is a growing number of studies, both British and American, which analyse the relationship between various aspects of social support and physical and psychological well-being in old age. Such well-being has been operationalised in ways which, if differing in detail, are broadly convergent; Challis (1981) and Davies and Knapp (1981), in particular, provide useful and sophisticated analyses of these concepts and their measurement. Challis' seven dimensions of need move from nurturance, or meeting of basic physical needs, through compensation for disability, independence, morale, social integration and family relationships to community development. Measurement is in terms of self care ability, including mobility (see Harris, 1971; and Townsend, 1979), intellectual impairment and psychological adjustment measured by such scales as the Philadelphia Geriatric Morale Scale. In addition, measures of social isolation (objective) (Townsend, 1963) and loneliness (subjective) (Wenger, 1984) are used. Although the various studies have used different criteria of need certain common themes do emerge. One is the psychological importance of social support, for the elderly as much as for other groups (see chapter 4, above). Thus Wenger (1981 and 1984) found an inverse correlation in North Wales between network size and both loneliness and morale (measured by the Philadelphia Scale) among the elderly - though poor health showed a closer connection with morale. Several earlier studies have shown a relationship between lack of social participation or/and social isolation and loneliness, anomia (Tunstall, 1966) or general life satisfaction (Abrams, 1978). The importance of having friends or/and neighbours and per contra the drawbacks of loneliness ranked very high in elderly people's assessments of the positive and negative aspects of their lives (Hunt, 1978, and Abrams, 1978).[1] These networks have been variously defined, but always include both kin and non-kin (see Mitchell and Trickett, 1980, for an indication of the range of definitions - and see below). In general, but particularly for working as opposed to middle class (Cochran et al., 1984) and possibly urban as opposed to rural populations (Walker, cited in Wenger, 1984, p.19) kin are more important than non-related people in terms of frequency and intensity of interaction, as well as for the provision of long-term, intensive physical care, or 'tending' (Parker, 1981). When relatives are non-existent or absent neighbours and friends often provide substitutes in terms of social support and, to a lesser degree, physical tending (Hunt, 1978).

Intensive physical care and supervision, though required only for that small proportion of elderly people who are appreciably or severely disabled, falls nearly always not only on kin, but on a member of the nuclear family and within that usually a woman (see chapter 8, above), with little support from other kin, friends or the state (see Parker, 1985). This realisation, together with the decreasing availability of female carers (due mainly to demographic changes and the increased proportion of women working - Parker, 1981), has recently stimulated research on the role of, and stresses on, carers (well reviewed in Parker, 1985 - see also chapter 1 above), but most conclusions at present need to be seen as tentative rather than firm. A pioneering study in this area was that of Isaacs and Neville (1974), which attempted to elucidate the factors making for undue stress on the carer or/and inadequate care for the person cared for. Though open to some criticism on methodological grounds this survey of 1035 old people in Strathclyde provides, we believe, valuable pointers towards an understanding of caring, and forms a basis for our analysis.

---

[1] Hunt found that the most frequent suggestion as to ways in which elderly people could be helped was 'voluntary helpers to chat, provide company' (answer given by 11% of elderly men, 12% of women) with 'regular medical, welfare visits' close behind (11% for both sexes). Of 'things liked', 'enjoys company of family, friends' came first, while loneliness came second only to poor health among things disliked. In Abrams' study the most important reason for satisfaction with one's life for those over 75 was 'good neighbours, good friends' - as might be expected this was particularly important for those living alone.

Social class – though not, except in some American studies, ethnicity [1] – has been important in analyses of social support: for example, middle class networks tend to be larger and more loosely-knit than those of the working class (Cochran et al., 1984; Eckenrode and Gore, 1981). This, though, is less stressed in the literature on the elderly. It has, however, been important in analyses of the use of the social and health services, where there is evidence that the middle class are at a decided advantage in hearing about the services on offer, and in making the most effective use of them (see Le Grand, 1982). Class position is widely seen as related to morbidity and mortality (see, for example, the Black Report, 1980). We shall make considerable use of class as an analytical variable in this and the two following chapters.

Geographical factors affect social support most obviously in terms of the physical distance between givers and recipients of aid, more generally in terms of geographical mobility both within the life-cycle, for example retirement migration (see Karn, 1977; and Wenger, 1984), and between generations. They are also relevant to the social structure of communities and neighbourhoods: Warren (1981) finds distinctive patterns of neighbourhood care in six different neighbourhood types in Detroit. In general, the stability of neighbourhoods, whether urban or rural, is correlated with dense networks (see Fischer, 1977, and 1982). Urban planning (see Jacobs, 1965) and housing policy (see McCafferty, 1985) appear to have an appreciable influence on social relationships.

Our discussion needs to incorporate some of the insights derived from the literature on the disabled, for a large proportion of the elderly are disabled; further, we are concerned with disabled people under pensionable age – excluding children. As mentioned above there is a large literature analysing perceptions of and reactions to disability – on the disabled person him/herself, the immediate carers, and the wider community as well as the professionals who bear the primary responsibility for defining the individual's condition. We take account of this in the ensuing analysis, especially in relation to stigma and segregation of the disabled (see Goffman, 1968; Blaxter, 1976; and Dartington et al., 1981). In addition the research findings on the relation between social networks and ill health (see Di Matteo and Hays, 1981; and Dingwall, 1976) are relevant. Such research suggests that social support has a generally positive effect on the patient's recovery and, as we have already seen (chapter 1), that one's social networks can affect willingness to seek professional help in the first place, sometimes negatively, sometimes positively.

After making some important comments about our sample and other interpretations of such concepts as 'disability', we intend to present a brief quantitative profile of the elderly and disabled in the sample in terms of type and degree of disability (if any), age, and household type. This is followed in the next two chapters by a rather more detailed analysis of their circumstances, and an account of the roles and problems of the carers which looks at their sources of help and

---

[1] Warren (1981) found black neighbourhoods in Detroit to play a more important role in help-seeking behaviour than white ones while Wenger (1984) introduces the distinction between native Welsh and 'incomers' (mainly from the English midlands) in her North Wales study. In our study, as in McCafferty's (1985), comparison is made between Protestants' and Catholics' frequency of contact with kin.

support, and the relation of these efforts to the formal sources of help. Lastly, an analysis is attempted of the factors affecting the interaction between helpers and helped, and an attempt is made to evaluate the effectiveness of caring and the cost to the carer and his/her family, utilising as a model Isaacs and Neville's study in Scotland (1974).

Before analysing the study data the relationship of these to the population from which they are drawn demands consideration. As has been stated (see chapter 2) the study was based on two samples, of which one (N=92) was designed to include specified quotas of elderly (70+) and disabled, the other to form a random sample of households in the village (N=100). Some comments need to be made:

(a) The combined samples cannot be seen as statistically representative of the population of the area; nevertheless as far as the elderly are concerned the discrepancy is not great – the proportion of those aged 60+ in the sample was 15 per cent, in the 1981 census 17 per cent. [1]

(b) The disabled were (deliberately) over-represented, and, in fact, a substantial proportion of the disabled population must have been covered: thus our study included a total of 86 slightly or appreciably disabled people [2] (in 72 households: three-eighths of N=192) while the OUTSET survey for Northern Ireland (OUTSET, 1982) found 86 'substantially impaired' people in the Glengow district. The equivalence of the two figures, which refer to different geographical areas and to disabilities of different degrees of severity is accidental, but does suggest that a relatively large sample has been obtained.

(c) The profile of ailments among the disabled in our study, with disabilities involving bones and organs of movement (about a quarter of all cases), the heart and circulatory system (about a sixth), and mental handicap (about an eighth) is sufficiently similar to what might be expected as to suggest that our sample is broadly representative of the disabled population (compare the Harris survey, 1971). It is probably unnecessary to elaborate on the problems inherent in attempts to measure the incidence of disability in a population: suffice it to say that the existence, still more the diagnosis, of disability as stated by the

---

[1] Census data quoted refer to rectangular areas defined by grid co-ordinates on the Ordnance Survey map (Small Area Statistics): the main areas used for this study have been (a) one including Glengow and the surrounding district, the latter corresponding to the area from which rural cases were taken – though such carers tended to be concentrated in certain parts of the area, as indicated in Table 2, above, and (b) the area of Glengow village. In the above comparison, and unless otherwise stated, figures given refer to (a).

[2] This figure includes some disabled children who are the subject of Ch.8. Figures relating to disabled persons given in this Chapter vary somewhat, depending on the availability of specific types of information.

individuals concerned, or/and their carers is subject to considerable variation, and the use of an initial postal survey as opposed to direct interviews is likely to lead to very different results (see ibid. Ch.1; and Townsend, 1979, Ch.20).

(d) Since household size and composition is relevant to the care given and received by the elderly/disabled it is worth comparing the survey data with those of the census (census data are available only on people of pensionable age in one and two person households). The figures are given for Glengow village only, as the great majority of the sample live there.

		Glengow Village		As % of total Population	
		Survey	Census	Survey	Census
Persons of pensionable age					
in 1-person	Male	3	11	0.6	0.9
household	Female	16	36	3.4	3.0
in 2-person household	Both sexes	21	72	4.5	5.9

Elderly people in two-person households (mainly the married, but also siblings or someone living with a child or other relative) are somewhat under-represented in our sample. The reasons for this are not clear but since the health and social circumstances of elderly married people are rather better than those of people living alone or in 'broken' households our survey may draw a slightly darker picture than is warranted. However, the discrepancies are not such as to make a substantial difference to our analysis.

In summary the data appear to provide a reasonable sampling of the survey population, though findings relating to sub-groups of the sample can clearly only suggest rather than prove hypotheses.

In addition to the data on disabled people in the sample households, data were obtained (in all but 31 cases) on disabled people among relatives outside the household and on others helped by someone in the household (Questions 7(b) in original sample questionnaire, and 10(b) and 12 in the PPRU survey questionnaire). A total of 59 persons (including 11 parents of sample heads of household) were mentioned, in 45 households. Because, unless they were being cared for by someone in one of the sample households, relatively little information was usually available about them, and because the great majority of them lived outside Glengow, the main part of these chapters is devoted to disabled people and to the elderly in the sample households themselves, though in a few instances data from these relatives' households are used, as appropriate.

The analysis of disability in terms of medical diagnoses [1] is less helpful for a sociological or social policy-orientated analysis than in

---

[1] In this survey, as in most large-scale studies of disability, the diagnosis is that of the respondent, not of a doctor, hence, from a medical point of view often imprecise and sometimes inaccurate.

terms of the individual's overall level of functioning and social context (see, for example, the Warnock Report, 1978, and Philip and Duckworth, 1982, pp.4-5). We shall focus, then:

(a) on the severity of disability, in terms of the individual's ability to cope unaided with the demands of everyday life, including self-care, mobility and such tasks as cooking and cleaning; and

(b) on the demands made on those who care for the disabled, in particular the level of onerousness represented by physical care, or tending.

These will be considered in relation to the composition of the disabled person's household, whose members normally constitute the principal human resources immediately available, to the wider social networks of which the individual is a part, and to the role of formal (statutory and voluntary) services and their relation to informal caring.

As the concepts used are vital for the analysis they require definition:

1   'Disability' is used here to refer to impairment of physical or mental abilities calculated to result in reduction in bodily or mental functioning; 'handicap' means the actual nett reduction in such functioning taking into account personality, social factors and aids of various kinds: thus a man who has lost a leg is severely disabled, but if he has an effective artificial limb and (say) a sedentary job may be minimally handicapped (see Harris, 1971, Ch.1). Except where otherwise stated we shall be basing our discussion on degrees of disability.   Three   grades   of   disability   are distinguished:

(1) slight, that is, involving difficulty or inability in carrying out relatively skilled, complex or strenuous activities, thus interfering with or preventing the performance of at least some of the individual's normal social or/and work roles: a person with a heart condition or mild mental retardation would fall into this category;

(2) appreciable, that is, preventing the individual from performing a considerable proportion of daily self-help activities, such as cooking and/or greatly reducing his/her mobility;

(3) severe, that is, preventing the individual from performing most, if not all of the most basic self-help activities, such as feeding or toileting oneself and/or rendering him/her completely or almost completely immobile: the bedfast, wheelchair users, the incontinent or/and severely mentally retarded individuals would be in this category.

2   'Tending' is a term coined by Parker (1981). His definition of it is 'such things as feeding, washing, lifting, cleaning up for the incontinent, protecting and comforting' as opposed to 'caring' (ibid, p.17). We would suggest that it is best defined as some form of physical care or/and home-making services, such as cooking, coupled with fairly close and constant supervision. The essential

elements are (a) rendering basic services for someone in respect of something which he/she is unable to perform unaided and (b) monitoring someone's welfare: 'comforting', of course, usually accompanies, but is analytically distinct from 'tending'. In terms of Parker's basic distinction we would in fact regard 'comforting' to be closer analytically to 'caring' rather than 'tending'.

Tending, like disability, may be divided into three levels, in terms of the onerousness, intimacy and basic nature of the services rendered. Thus:

Level 1 refers to such services as cooking or cleaning, giving lifts or shopping (Isaacs and Neville's, 1974, short-interval and long-interval needs);

Level 2 to helping someone to dress or helping them up or down stairs, together with some more intimate help;

Level 3 to the full range of tending of a completely incapacitated person, including all the processes of feeding, bathing and toileting (critical-interval needs).

The degree of supervision (general or constant) required in relation to a mentally confused person may also enter into the definition.

Disability and tending are, of course, related but are not homologous; thus those with slight disability will often not require 'tending' at all (for example, a patient with stabilised cancer or non-florid mental illness) because daily intervention by another person is not required.

3   'Households' are classified as:

single person;

two person: either husband and wife or two siblings

'ordinary' families: a marital couple plus their child or children;

'broken' family households: a non-married (usually widowed but also divorced, deserted or never-married) head of household (HOH), with one or more non-married younger relatives, for example, a son, daughter or niece, sometimes with a child or children of one of these relatives;

'complex': an 'ordinary' family as above with one or more relatives (usually widowed) of the same or an older generation to HOH.

This classification may be compared with that given in chapter 3 above (derived from Fox, 1978); the two of course overlap but serve rather different purposes.

4   'Networks' refer to individuals with whom a given person (ego) has a social relationship and the relationships (if any) between these people. Networks include both kin and non-kin, although much fuller information is available in this study on the former. In operational as well as theoretical terms the limits of networks are

difficult to define - one of Boissevain's (1974) informants claimed a network of over 2,000 people - but two major criteria for inclusion are frequency of contact and importance in ego's life (Mitchell, 1969, p.2 argues that the links between ego and people in the network must be such as can be used to interpret the social behaviour of the persons involved and Whitten and Wolfe, 1973, p.720 refer to linkages 'which may form a basis for the mobilization of people for specific purposes'). Not all those one talks to frequently are important in one's life, conversely old friends living in another country to whom one writes once a year may still be important. Different people may of course, be important for different purposes, or in different contexts. In the discussion that follows the 'total' is distinguished from the 'effective' network, the latter including relatives and friends with whom ego is in regular, frequent contact and/or who 'rally round' in a crisis, such as illness or bereavement.

It is evident that these categories are inevitably somewhat arbitrary: nevertheless they do provide fruitful devices for exploring the data, since fairly gross distinctions are sufficient for most of the purposes of the analysis.

Now we can turn to our sample. We are concerned in this analysis with three groups:

Old people (60 years and over), who are also disabled. This group is made up of 46 persons (16 male, 30 female);

Old people who are not disabled: 42 (20 male, 22 female);

Disabled adults (18 years plus) under the age of 60: 22 (12 male, 10 female).

Of the disabled 43 have been categorised as disability level one and 25 have been categorised as disability levels two and three.

Analysis of the data in terms of sex, age, household composition and marital status suggests a number of conclusions which, though necessarily tentative, tend to reflect well-established demographic trends or previous research (such as Harris, 1971, p.5):

1   There are relatively more women aged 70+ than men: men generally die younger than women.

2   Women are more likely to be disabled than men, not only overall (65% vs. 58%) but also at each age level, the difference increasing with age (70+: 61% women vs 40% men disabled). On the other hand, nearly half the male disabled, but only a quarter of the women, were under 60.

3   Further, at each age (except under 60) and overall (53% vs. 31%), a higher proportion of women are appreciably or severely disabled.

4   More than half the women are widowed, whereas the majority of men are still married.

5   There were more single (never-married) men than women, but they
    were much less likely to live alone (five out of ten single men
    lived with unmarried siblings).

6   Disabled men were likely to be living with their wives, disabled
    women to be widows, living in 'broken' or 'complex' households.
    No less than nine disabled women over 60, of whom five were
    appreciably or severely disabled lived alone. No disabled men
    did so. It follows that men were most likely to be cared for by
    their wives, women by their daughters, sons or daughters-in-law.
    Conversely, male carers were likely to be caring for their
    wives, women carers for women of an older generation,
    particularly their mothers, or mothers-in-law. Analysis in
    terms of severity of disability indicates that the former group
    tend to be less disabled, and the latter more. Thus men's
    experience of caring will be appreciably different from that of
    women.

7   Overall there were more female than male 'principal carers',
    defined as the person who bore the main - sometimes the sole-
    responsibility for a disabled person. In most but not all cases
    this person was also a 'tender' as defined above. This, of
    course, was likely to be true where disability was more severe,
    and in this category women predominated even more. Thus of 27
    people tending 23 cases (at levels two and three) five were men
    (shared tending in three cases), 16 women and six in the
    statutory or 'commercial' sectors.

9 Disability and old age: 2

The more severely disabled and those tending them must concern the student of social policy most, both in terms of the needs of the disabled themselves and in terms of the burdens placed on their carers. These inter-related sets of needs and the ways they are met are analysed by Isaacs and others, in their studies of the elderly and disabled in Strathclyde (1972 and 1974). On the basis of their analysis they evaluate each situation in terms of 'defendedness' or 'defeat'. A 'defended' case is one where both the basic needs of the disabled person are being met and the principal carer is neither under strain of such severity that his or her well-being is seriously affected nor that an imminent breakdown in caring is threatened.[1] 'Defeat' means that one or both of these conditions are unfulfilled. These concepts are utilised in the discussion that follows.

------

[1] Isaacs and Neville's definition (1974, p.23) of 'insufficient basic care' was that 'the subject was deprived, for part or all of the day or night, of a satisfactory standard of food, warmth, cleanliness or security'; and of 'undue stress' on the carer as 'when the physical, psychological or social well-being of the helper was threatened by the care of the subject'. This definition did not include, but their discussion implied, potential breakdown of caring.

As before, though they are operationalised in a rather impressionistic way, such concepts do provide a sufficiently accurate if crude yardstick of success or failure. (The fact that a much smaller proportion of the Glengow than of the large Strathclyde sample are recorded as 'defeated' reflects, we believe, not measurement error but more effective help both from informal and statutory sources in Glengow).[1] Because we lay particular stress on the problems of carers, or, in relation to the more or less severely disabled people, 'tenders', we analyse the data in terms of the problems facing the tenders, not the disabled.

In order to explore the interplay of relevant factors and to present as much as possible of the evidence on which our conclusions will be based it is necessary to present the material in considerable detail. To summarise and clarify the data it is presented first in tabular form, in terms of four categories of tending:

1   statutory and 'commercial' tenders

2   women tending husbands

3   male tenders and

4   women tenders in 'broken' and 'complex' households.

GROUP ONE: STATUTORY AND 'COMMERCIAL' TENDERS

It is noticeable that those in receipt of help from 'private' or statutory tenders (Group One) were all one-person households (except for the living-in 'companion') and that they had few kin (case 104 being a notable exception), or few who were able and/or willing to help.   In terms of the criteria for providing home helps, this is hardly surprising (see, for example, McCoy, 1982; Wenger, 1984, p.117).   It is interesting, however, that this group tends to enjoy an appreciable degree of neighbourly support, and in one case, a friend is listed as a co-principal carer with the home help.   The substitution of neighbourly for absent kin help has been noted in the literature on the elderly (see Hunt, 1978).   So one case, Mrs Nelson (126), who suffers from varicose veins and leg ulcers, receives help from an elderly neighbour, Mr Baines, who is clearly what Collins and Pancoast (1976) call a 'natural helping person':   he brings in the coal for her, sometimes washes her feet, 'sees her to bed' and locks up at night.   The greater part of her needs (she cannot walk, except with a walking frame) are, however, met by a thrice-daily, seven days a week, home help.   Mrs Nelson says all her siblings and her late husband's siblings are dead;   she has a married daughter in Birmingham, another whose address is unknown, and a step-son in a town twelve miles away.   She herself comes from about twenty miles away.

---

[1] The Strathclyde study is on a much larger scale than our own and is only in general terms comparable with it, hence no elaborate comparison is attempted. However, of their total sample of 1035, 63 had 'critical interval' potential need (approximately equivalent to our severely disabled), and of these 36 were 'defended', 27 'defeated'. Our data show only two 'defeated' out of 22 where the level of tending is graded 2 or 3.

GROUP ONE: STATUTORY AND 'COMMERCIAL' TENDERS

Q'aire Number	Nature of H'Hold	Tending Score	Relation of tender to person tended	Disability	Age of person tended	Other Principal Carer(s)	Secondary Carer(s)	Social Support Network	Stress on Carer (0-3)	Situation Defended or Defeated or Borderline (+)(++) (-)(--) (+-)
216 [1]	1-p	3	Home Help	Legs amputated, etc.	72	Friend	Very limited	Decidedly limited: few relatives	-	+
104	HOH+W Companion	2	Companion	Broken hip, deaf, confused	81	-	Miss Bryce and other relatives	Good	-	++
122	HOH+W Companion	2/3	Companion	Arthritis	89	-	Cleaner; relatives	Medium	-	++
126	1-p	3	Home Help	Leg Ulcer etc.	70+	District Nurse	Tom Baines and other neighbours	Limited kin, and neighbours	-	+
020	1-p	1/2	Home Help	Epilepsy, arthritis, ulcer, etc.	67	-	-	Limited kin, and neighbours	-	+

[1] In this chapter the convention will be followed of referring to cases by questionnaire numbers only, except where a detailed account or verbatim quotation is given.

GROUP TWO: WIVES

Q'aire Number	Nature of H'Hold	Tending Score	Relation of tender to person tended	Disability	Age of person tended	Other Principal Carer(s)	Secondary Carer(s)	Social Support Network	Stress on Carer (0-3)	Situation Defended (+)(++) or Defeated (-)(—) or Borderline (+-)
003	H+W	2/3	Wife	Angina, arthritis	75	-	Daughter	Medium to good	1/2	+-
050	H+W+ ch'n	2	Wife	Cancer	?	-	-	Good	1	?
261	H+W?	2/3	Wife	Stroke	78	Daughter	Other daughter, other relatives	Good	0	+ (++?)
113	H+W	2	Wife	Stroke	71	-	-	Limited to medium	0/1	+

GROUP THREE: MALE TENDERS

Q'aire Number	Nature of H'Hold	Tending Score	Relation of tender to person tended	Disability	Age of person tended	Other Principal Carer(s)	Secondary Carer(s)	Social Support Network	Stress on Carer (0-3)	Situation Defended (+)(++) or Defeated (-)(—) or Borderline (+-)
042	H+W	3	Husband	Stroke: deteriorating	60s	None	Daughter, nurse, home help	Medium	1/2	+ (but may become - in future)
283	H+W+ adult ch'n	2	Husband	Nervous disorder (partly in wheel-chair)	61	Daughter	Son (in house)	Limited (no close relatives)	1	+-
006	Siblings	1/2	Brother	Chest, eyesight, hearing	60s	Sister	-	Appears limited	0/1	+-
220	'Broken'	3	Son	Multiple sclerosis	66	None	Carer's sister (or/+ statutory help)	Medium to poor (3 relatives closish touch)	2	-
263	1-p	2	Brother-in-law	Disabled since birth	63	Home Help	-	?	-	

GROUP FOUR: WOMEN TENDERS IN 'BROKEN' AND 'COMPLEX' HOUSEHOLDS

Q'aire Number	Nature of H'Hold	Tending Score	Relation of tender to person tended	Disability	Age of person tended	Other Principal Carer(s)	Secondary Carer(s)	Social Support Network	Stress on Carer (0-3)	Situation Defended (+)(++) or Defeated (-)(--) or Borderline (+-)
015	HOH+ad. D.	1/2	Daughter	Deaf, frail	V. old	-	?	?	?	?
043	HOH+non-married sons	2	Mother	Down's syndrome	26	-	-	Good	1	+
107	HOH+ad. D.	3	Daughter	Heart, arthritis, ulcer, etc.	76	-	Neighbour, cousin	Medium	2/3	-
287	HOH+ niece	3	Niece	Burns on leg	83	-	District nurse	Limited	1	+
056	HW, +ch'n +WZ, HM	2	Son's wife	Parkinson's disease	85	-	Pte. home help, nurses, etc.	Good	1	+
105	HW, +ch'n HM	3	Son's wife	Heart, bronchitis, asthma	80	-	Son, grand-daughter	Good	1	++
025	HW+ch'n +H cousin	3	Cousin's wife	Senile	80	-	Cousin (carer's H) housekeeper	Good	2	+
223	HW+ch'n +HZ	1/2	Brother's wife	Blind, frail, skin	52	-	Brothers and other siblings, etc. Social Worker	Strong network	1	+

Another old lady, Mrs Jackson (72 years) (case 216), who had both legs amputated some years ago, has a woman friend who provides (unspecified) help and a home help (the same one as Mrs Nelson) thrice-daily, seven days a week. Also a widow, she comes originally from a farm about six miles away, and has been only four years in Glengow. She has no children: a few of her husband's relatives live in a town about twenty miles to the south but she hardly ever sees them. Like Mrs Nelson, she lives in a 'close' of Housing Executive accommodation.

A contrast to these two people is the widow of a well-off farmer (Mrs Johnson, case 104, above), now living in town in her own good-sized house in the main street. She has a large circle of brothers and nieces – as well as a woman friend of over 50 years standing – who effectively co-ordinate their efforts on her behalf. She also has a woman neighbour (who had previously worked as a home help for her) who puts on the fire and locks up and so forth each day, and her current daily home help. However, by the end of the study her brother had arranged for a live-in companion. She has a broken hip joint, is partly deaf and suffers from mild intermittent mental confusion.

Thanks mainly to the provision of quite intensive service from statutory/commercial sources, and the fact that, though fairly severely disabled, they are all (save, in part, Mrs Johnson) mentally alert and not incontinent, these five women may all be categorised as 'defended'. With one exception (a single woman of 60 who is 'very lonely and depressed' – she does have relatives but they only visit for a quarter of an hour on a Sunday) they also appear to be reasonably happy.

GROUP TWO: WOMEN TENDING HUSBANDS

The four married men cared for by their wives, and sometimes daughters, are rather less severely disabled than the previous group discussed and they and their carers are supported by fairly effective social networks, mainly kin. Their situation may, however, put appreciable stress on caring wives, who are sometimes unwell. Mrs Anderson (003), for example, the same age (75) as her husband, who has long-standing angina and also severe arthritis, herself suffers from high blood pressure. Although she has very helpful neighbours, one of whom takes her the three miles into Glengow to shop once a week, and another who helped get her husband back to bed on one occasion, she is seldom able to leave him. This case has been categorised as on the borderline between 'defended' and 'defeated': it is clear that the carer's life is considerably circumscribed, and it is unlikely that things can go on much longer without sharply increasing stress.

GROUP THREE: MALE TENDERS

As was pointed out above, most male tenders are tending less severely disabled people than are women tenders. However, in this section, which deals with the more severe cases, the difficulties of men in tending are at least as great as those of women who are caring for their husbands; they have a less onerous task, though, than young women caring for older relatives (Group 4). In two cases the relative cared for is a wife, in two others a brother (this is a two-sibling household) and brother-in-law, and in probably the most stressful case, a mother. The persons cared for were all in their 60s – over a decade younger, on average,

than husbands cared for by wives, but more severely disabled.
Considerable help was provided by female relatives (sisters or
daughters); and in two cases by a home help and in one a nurse. This
bears out the point we make elsewhere that greater statutory as well as
informal help is made available for male carers. The level of stress
among the carers, one of whom is 12 years older than his wife, is fairly
high, and the margin between defendedness and defeat tends to be small.

One husband, Mr O'Connell (042), has had the care of a wife with a
stroke for 28 years. He receives help from his daughter who lives
nearby and visits often; his wife's brother also visits. A nurse comes
every few days as does a home help. Mr O'Connell, however, clearly
faces a heavy and increasing burden. Just 'defended', the case may well
become 'defeated' in the future.

Under heavier pressure, and recorded as defeated, is the unmarried 35
year old son caring for a widowed mother of 66 years suffering from
multiple sclerosis (Mrs Morrison). He has a married brother and sister
both living within about four miles, who visit at least weekly, but the
physical tending devolves almost entirely on him. An electrician by
trade, he is unemployed (one can only speculate whether this was in
order to care for his mother). He has seen someone 'from the welfare'
but has heard nothing further. He would welcome a range of services for
his mother (Q.14c in the PPRU questionnaire), indeed all those listed,
except a night nurse. At present, only financial help is available, and,
according to the interviewer, he is a bit depressed with the constant
care and attention. Interestingly, this man has lived in Glengow all
his life, 10 years at the same address, but seems very isolated. This
person seems to correspond in all but his sex to the faithful spinster
daughter stereotype, but as the case was part of the PPRU sample no
further details are available to interpret the situation.

Jack Bond, a forestry worker in his 60s, is caring for a brother
Charles of approximately the same age who has been on social security
benefit for 20 years, and has 'chest trouble', bad eyesight and
deafness. There is evidently only one close relative, a sister living
about three miles away who, however, visits daily. This type of menage
is not uncommon in the countryside around Glengow: there are other
examples in the original sample of bachelor siblings living together,
perhaps a product of the same sort of factors that have produced an
excess of bachelors in rural Ireland as a whole.

GROUP FOUR: WOMEN TENDERS IN 'BROKEN' AND 'COMPLEX' HOUSEHOLDS

Group Four is composed of 'broken' households as well as 'complex' ones:
eight cases in all. In the first category, carers were all blood-
relations: a mother, two daughters and a niece; in the second, they
were all related only by marriage, i.e., the husband's mother, cousin or
sister had come to live in the household. One of the 'broken' families
contained as the severely disabled person a 26 year old son, Jimmy
Henaghan (043) with Down's Syndrome (tending score of two) who attended
an adult training centre, a less severely subnormal son of 36 who 'helps
out', a normal son separated from his wife, and the mother (tender) of
about 68, who suffered from high blood pressure. This case, which we
have met before (chapter 5) illustrates well the willingness on the
tender's part to shoulder a heavy burden cheerfully: 'I had a hard time
rearing him but it was worth it all: he's come out of it rightly'. It

also illustrates the close texture of kin support, mainly from Mrs Henaghan's late husband's brothers and grown-up offspring, especially Jimmy's nearest brother Tom (27 years) who is 'very attached to Jimmy, very good, very attentive'. With help from social services (the Day Centre) and close practical as well as emotional support, this case is clearly 'defended' despite the tender's age and frailty. Several relatives live in close proximity to this rural family, some of whom provide help.

Of the other seven families, one respondent (015), provided too little information to permit an analysis: she is 'very old' and deaf, and lives with a widowed daughter in Housing Executive accommodation in a hamlet near Glengow. Another elderly lady (case 287), a retired shopkeeper of 83 years, reports all her close family as dead. Though 'more or less chairbound at present', due to leg injuries, it seems her disability is of short duration. A niece who has come to look after her 'as long as her aunt needs her' does an estimated 33 hours per week tending, and the district nurse comes to dress the leg and to help with the bathing.

A fourth 'broken' household, which well illustrates the range of pressures falling on a devoted daughter, is that of Mrs Barker (107), which was described at the beginning of this chapter. This case is in part parallel to that of the 35 year old son caring for his mother (above) but seems both more severe (the mother, with multiple disabilities, heart disease, arthritis, ulcer, etc. in fact died during the course of the research) and also to have appreciably more help and support, from kin and neighbours (as mentioned, in two cases neighbours were kin) as well as the health services (regular calls by a nurse). Although Mary – there is also a brother in the house, who is in employment – did not complain, this situation could have been classified as 'defeated', and the stress on the carer 'objectively', at least, was very great. The burden seems to have been borne not only bravely, but willingly. It may be relevant that Mary probably had few prospects of marriage and none of job advancement by the time she had to return home: she seemed to ask rather little of life.

The group of 'complex' families contained disabled people, three out of four in their eighties, who were severely handicapped and who imposed potentially a very considerable level of stress on carers who were all only relatives by marriage. Nevertheless all have been listed as 'defended'. Three characteristics common to all or most of the situations, are, it is suggested, responsible for this appreciable degree of success. First, despite the severity of the illnesses (for example, Parkinson's disease, blindness) only in one case (senility) did they preclude some degree of positive response, in the form of reciprocation. Second, though two of the male household heads had manual jobs these were skilled and stable ones, and in general all four in various respects enjoyed some affluence.[1] Thus one was able to hire a private home help and another a housekeeper to cope with the extra demands of the disabled relative. In the latter case the tender in fact had a professional job (lawyer) and was not prepared to give it up. The majority of the children in this group, if of age, had experienced tertiary education. Thirdly, all four families had strong social support from a range of relatives and friends: a higher level of support, in fact, than any of the other groups with high tending scores.

---

[1] The Attendance Allowance was important, however.

These families (three Protestant, one Catholic) are part of well-established networks of farming, professional or at least skilled families in the area - though some relatives live as far afield as Belfast, Edinburgh and New Zealand. One of those families (Mr Thompson's) has also been analysed at the beginning of the Chapter. In general the family were able to cope satisfactorily with the elder Mrs Thompson, without major detriment to their family and social life. They have been categorised as very well defended.

The Clarks (025) represent a less satisfactory situation. This family and Mrs Clark's relations with her husband's cousin, Ethel Murphy, have been discussed in chapter 5 but will be briefly analysed here. Although Mrs Clark had met Mrs Murphy on occasional visits 'home' to Northern Ireland from abroad, and evidently Mr Clark felt grateful to her for previous kindnesses, the relationship was much less close, both genealogically and in terms of contact, than that of Mrs Thompson with her husband's mother. Mrs Clark's children, who ranged from 4 to 13 years - and a fourth baby was born a couple of weeks after the first interview - were if anything in a competitive rather than a co-operative relationship to Mrs Clark's tending for Mrs Murphy. Further, while the younger Mrs Thompson had worked for only a part of her married life, and as a shop assistant, Mrs Clark was a lawyer. Although she and her husband had a close kin network and many friends, they did not in fact receive much effective help from them. Above all, Mrs Murphy's senility and her incontinence were, as stressed in chapter 6, major sources of stress. It seems that, despite Mrs Clark's courage and determination, and the (mainly) moral support of her husband, the burden was heavy; however, it was not such as to cause a breakdown in caring, hence this situation has been classified as 'defended'.

We now turn to a discussion of those with relatively few, or no, disabilities.

The slightly disabled, both those requiring 'tending' and those able to function satisfactorily on their own form the next group to be analysed. Since the problems they and those who care for them face are much less severe than in the group just analysed, the focus will be not on the stress on carers, or on the 'defeated/defended' dichotomy (or, more accurately, continuum) but on the support they receive. In general, however, this group requires a less detailed analysis than that of the more severely disabled.

There are 24 women and 23 men in the group, of whom 12 of each sex are classified as requiring tending (at Grade 1, the lowest level of onerousness). Four cases, where a disabled son lives with his parents or widowed mother, might have been categorised with handicapped children, though the age group is 18 to 36. Two of these are mentally handicapped (one of them a brother of the severely handicapped young man mentioned above, Jimmy Henaghan); one diabetic; and one suffering from multiple sclerosis.

In socio-demographic terms, the group may be divided basically into three sub-groups for each sex:

WOMEN: 6 living alone, 10 with husbands, with or without children, and 5 in broken or complex households. There are also two unmarried sisters living together.

MEN: One living alone, 11 in ordinary nuclear families, and 4 in
           broken or complex families. There are two pairs of bachelors,
           and a brother and sister pair.

It is clear that many more of the slightly disabled than of the
severely disabled are living with husband or wife and relatively fewer
in broken or complex households. It follows that the context of caring
or tending is likely to be different - not only less onerous - than in
the case of the majority of the severely disabled: this is especially
true of women as several men are caring for severely disabled wives.

The one-person households are noteworthy for being composed almost
entirely of women, of whom most are widowed (3) or separated (1), the
others single. Most of those living on their own had smallish networks
(a phenomenon noted in the Dinnington study) [1] and were classified as
poor: two had been domestic servants, one a factory worker and one a
school cleaner (and farmer's wife). Three of the six women complained
of 'nerves' (2) or 'depression' (1) - neurosis was disproportionately
concentrated in this group. Two of the failures to complete inter-
viewing were within this group; one terminated the interview after about
a quarter of an hour, the other was reluctant to give the first, and
declined a follow-up interview. This latter woman seemed to associate
the researcher with 'the welfare' which had just refused an application
for help. Apart from the trauma of her own marriage break-up, one of
the women had had to leave her daughter's home because the latter and
her husband had split up.

Help provided for these individuals came respectively from a daughter
plus a neighbour (who cuts the grass), in another two cases from
daughters, in one from a son and in another from a 'natural helping
person' in Springdale. One had a home help.

To summarise, the members of this small group are poor, have rather
limited social resources and receive perhaps limited help from statutory
services. In some cases they suffer from social or/and psychological
problems. With the exception of Mr Arnold, the only man in the group,
they have moved to Glengow village and to their present addresses only
within the last few years. The distance moved, though, has been
relatively small - the longest move being about 15 miles.

Turning to those who are married, men slightly outnumber women and, in
accordance with a tendency of the male disabled to be younger than the
female, are disproportionately under 60. Most of the men, but rather
fewer of the women, appear to have large networks. The married include
a range of socio-economic statuses, but are generally better off than
those in one-person households. One elderly couple, with several
children and many grandchildren, indicated their financial status in,
among other ways, the listing of large farms owned by their sons. There
is a range of afflictions, with arthritis and angina predominating.

There are two pairs of unmarried brothers, one brother and sister
household, and one pair of sisters. All except the last pair are
classified as poor and their networks are medium to limited. None has a
car. The two pairs of brothers live on farms, further exemplifying the
surplus of men (and, indeed, bachelors) in general on farms - especially

---

[1] Bayley, M. et al., 1985, pp.9-12.

small farms - in Northern Ireland (noted, for a broadly similar area, by Edwards, 1981 - 37% of farms he studied were 'overmanned'). One of the brothers (described by his family as 'oddish') is slightly mentally handicapped but not severely so, and consequently required some care from the brother with whom he lives.

The slightly disabled were much less likely than the severely disabled to be in 'complex' households; only one such household was found among males (the husband's brother, who suffered from arthritis, lived with the family) and one among females (Mrs Thompson, carer for her severely disabled mother-in-law, referred to above, who herself developed angina). Three 'broken' households were constituted by disabled widows with adult children, while in the two male cases it was the adult sons who were disabled. No clear common characteristic was observed among the broken or complex cases except that the former all contained disabilities requiring Grade One tending (e.g., arthritis with sciatica, multiple sclerosis and 'nerves'), and that the broken families were rather worse off (working class or poor) and the complex ones better off (working or middle), a tendency noted in relation to the more severely disabled (see chapter 8).

In general, men are relatively more in evidence as tenders or carers (in a number of cases 'tending' as such is not required) in these relatively easy situations than when tending is more onerous. Thus we have in this group some 11 husbands, 4 sons and 2 brothers, total 17, as against 12 wives, 1 brother's wife, 3 daughters, 1 grand-daughter, 4 sisters and 3 mothers, total 24. The relatively greater male contribution is related partly to the fact that there are many more married couples one (or occasionally, both) of whom is slightly disabled than there are among the more severely disabled.

We now move on to consider the fit elderly; those aged 60 and over who are not recorded as disabled in any way. It is striking that these 44 individuals (20 men and 24 women) are by no means only in the younger old age groups: 17 are 70 or over and 2 (men) in their 80s. A few of them, it should be noted, are caring for disabled wives, husbands and other relatives.

Seven women and four men live on their own; five of the former, but only one of the latter are widowed (the other three men had never married). The men appear to have rather smaller networks than the women, though three women, two of whom had come to Glengow recently (or returned after living away for a number of years) had small ones - the smallest of these was constituted by a sister of 85 in a seaside town, last seen four months before and a daughter in Canada. One of the women (aged 71) who lived in a terrace of old people's flats formed part of what was evidently a considerable, fairly close-knit, working class network of kin (especially on the husband's side) and probably neighbours. In addition she quoted in reply to Question 15 (to whom she would turn if 'down' or ill) the names of a woman for whom she worked as a home help and the daughter of another client - a clear illustration of the informal penumbra of a supposedly formal service, as well as of (at least potential) reciprocity.

Fourteen elderly men but only nine elderly women lived with their spouses (the difference is explained by the fact that some spouses were under 60) and in about half these cases with one or more children. None of the men lived in 'broken' but two lived in 'complex' households: one was a 74 year old widower, the other an 86 year old single man, uncle of the female head of household. Of the women, four lived in broken households and two in complex ones.

Following the now familiar pattern, most of those married had medium to large networks, though two 'complex' households (in both of which the wife was disabled) had smallish ones. Those married tended to be of higher socio-economic status than those living alone and than the women in broken or complex households.

Five of those in 'broken' or 'complex' households are classified as poor, only one as 'working class', but they tended to have large social networks. Three of them were, in fact, part of the same network: one which - composed mainly of households headed by unskilled or semi-skilled manual workers, several of whom were unemployed, and located largely in two socially similar sections - appears to exemplify the Bott and Institute of Community Studies type of dense, working class network (see Bott, 1971; and Young and Willmott, 1962).

A large majority of the non-disabled elderly were either born and brought up in Glengow or had lived most of their lives there; those who had moved in had usually come from farms or hamlets within a few miles. This compares with the disabled, who had usually moved from rather further away.

With few exceptions the above data suggest that these elderly but fit people had adequate immediate social support and were part of quite substantial, mostly kin networks. Insofar as the great majority of them had lived in Glengow for most, if not all, of their lives, they can be assumed to be well integrated in community terms (see Timms, 1983; Biegel and Naparstek, 1982). In other words, they were 'at home' in the village even if there is only limited evidence of participation in organised activities. The churches were by far the most important focus of such activities though some elderly women remained members of the Women's Institute. Though most of the fit elderly were working class or 'poor' there is little obvious evidence of unmet need.

There were a few cases which appeared more or less isolated, in particular the three women living alone already mentioned. It is of interest that one of these (aged 63) was herself caring for her own mother, who was in poor health and lived a mile or two out of town: perhaps caring itself may give meaning and solace to life, though unfortunately we lack detail from the subject in this case (PPRU survey). In addition, two of the single men and two of the married had limited networks.

At the risk of some over-simplification it may be worth trying to summarise some of the salient features of the elderly/disabled as discussed in this chapter as follows:

Degree of Disability

Household Type	Appreciable/ Severe	Slight	None
Complex	Sex: female Class: higher Networks: large Functioning: good	Sex: both Class: rather higher	Sex: both Class: low Networks: large

Broken	Sex: female
	Class: lower
	Networks: often
	    smaller
	Functioning: only
	    fair
		Sex: both
		Class: somewhat
		    lower
			Sex: female
			Class: low
			Networks: large

Married	Sex: male
	Networks: medium
	    to large
	Social service
	help to male
	carers
	Functioning: fair
	(female) to good
	(male)
		Sex: both
		Class: wide
		    range
			Sex: both
			Networks: medium
			    to large

Single person	Class: low
	Networks: small
	Social service
	help to 1-person
	households (and
	unmarried
	siblings)
	Functioning: good
		Sex: female
		    mostly
		Class: low
		Networks: small,
		singles tend to
		be immigrants
			Sex: female
			    mostly
			Networks: vary,
			mostly established
			in Glengow

This presentation serves to highlight issues of sex, social class and network size. The following chapter endeavours to provide a detailed analysis of these, and other, factors.

10 Disability and old age: 3

As indicated in the previous chapter, we now attempt an overall view of
the care given to the disabled and elderly in Glengow. The main point
to make is that the kinship system provides a high level of caring. Our
study has identified many tenders who were making considerable efforts
to help their elderly disabled relatives in the community, for example,
Mary Barker (107), Mrs Carter (052), Mrs Rivers (223) and especially,
perhaps, Mrs Clark. Several people in fact expressed explicit
opposition to putting their elderly relatives in an old people's home or
other institution: the Clarks were given this choice by a hospital
consultant but declined. Further, several elderly wives and one or two
husbands (not analysed above because the incidents concerned were in the
past) had nursed their husband or wife devotedly for many years before
he or she died. One elderly lady, Mrs Davidson, for example, had a
husband who died of gangrene in the leg. Though she had nursing help
each day, she was up with her husband much of each night. Her son
advised her to put his father in hospital but she said: 'He just wanted
nobody but me to attend to him, you know, so I thought, what about it,
I'll get over it'. Neighbourly efforts to prevent admission to an old
people's home are exemplified by one case (237) when the female
respondent (Mrs Brownlow) mentions helping a neighbour (Mr Granger),
presumably living on his own, by shopping and cooking for him. She
commented: 'He's very popular and everyone helps him. He shouldn't be
put in an old people's home as he can get about still'.

The stress involved in tending elderly relatives varied from some
limitation on the carer's movements, for example, the case of a woman
with a very old but hale uncle of her father (case 052), to virtual
imprisonment in the home, for example, the Barker case (107). In the
Barker case this was coupled with the complete range of physical tending
of a very sick (and very heavy) woman day and night. Perhaps

surprisingly, in view of the literature (for example, Nissel and Bonnerjea, 1982; E.O.C., 1980), there was very little evidence of deterioration in health as a result of caring. That Mrs Thompson developed angina just after her mother-in-law died is the only case of this. Possibly the size of the sample was too small to pick up other instances. Parker's (1981) 'dimensions' of 'tending' (namely duration, intensity, complexity and prognosis) would seem to apply to a number of cases of severe disability in this study. So too does Isaacs and Neville's (1974) point about the especially severe burden imposed by incontinence or/and mental confusion - the former is related to intensity, the latter (since confusion in the elderly is progressive) to prognosis. In the cases that have been classified as borderline or as clearly defeated, two or more of Parker's factors were negative: tending was an intensive activity in, for example, the cases of Clark, Barker, Anderson and Barnard, and it was clear in each instance that the person tended was almost certain to get worse, either gradually or in terms of a sudden crisis. Duration of disability/illness was comparatively short (3 years) in Clark's case, longer in the others.

The factors enabling tenders or carers to continue functioning and to do so effectively are partly to do with the nature of the illness/disability, partly with the socio-economic position of the household. Affluence on the one hand and poverty on the other have a wide range of direct as well as indirect effects on the situation of tender and disabled, ranging as noted above from money to pay for a full-time living-in companion to lack of information about benefits and lack of confidence in claiming them (a number of instances of this were encountered).

More germane to the main theme of this study is the factor of social support. It has been shown, in relation to the more severely disabled, that large networks and defended situations were correlated. [1] This appeared to be particularly true in the case of complex families, despite the fact that the presence of a non-member of the nuclear family in the household is likely to be a cause of stress. On the other hand, both for the severely and the slightly disabled, small networks, one-person, and to some extent, broken households and low levels of defence, or at least poor functioning, were also correlated.

The establishment of a relationship between networks and successful functioning needs to be supplemented by an analysis of how it operates. The fairly intensive nature of much of the interviewing, and the understanding provided through participant observation, permit us to offer a number of fairly well-founded suggestions as to the processes involved.

Firstly, where there are 'effective' relatives as well as friends and neighbours, direct assistance with physical tending and with the meeting of short-interval needs, such as cooking, or of 'long interval' needs, such as shopping, is often available (though less so in the case of tending). [2] A very good example is Mrs Johnson's situation before she had a companion (cited above): the complementarity of the efforts of

---

[1] Compare Wenger, 1984

[2] Townsend's research (1963, p.87) confirmed the commonsense expectation that total contacts rise with number of children.

six or seven secondary carers - the primary carers were, in effect, the home help, and, to some extent, the neighbour - was in a degree formalised by a 'family council of war' held, interestingly enough, shortly after the researcher's visit. Similarly, in the case of Mrs Rivers (the carer) it appears that the care of Miss Rivers, a disabled person, in effect rotated among different siblings - even if bitter complaints were heard to the effect that this process worked 'jerkily' and imperfectly, so that she tended to 'get stuck' too long with one relative. Miss Barker (107) was, very temporarily, relieved of the care of her mother so that she could go shopping. It remains true, though, as many researchers have pointed out (for example, Bayley, 1973; E.O.C. 1980), that such help is generally indirect. The principal tender is seldom relieved of much of the burden of actual physical care.

Secondly, and more subtly, the web of relatives and/or friends does provide psychological support for both the carer and the cared for, and an endorsement of his or her efforts (Wenger, 1984, p.183). It is impossible to quantify or even clearly to demonstrate this: it is at least implicit, for example, in the remarks by Mary Barker about her aunt's distress that, because she herself was ill, she could not 'do anything' about her sick sister; and also in the distress of a cousin when she heard (tardily) of Mrs Barker's illness. A friend who gave Mary Barker an outing to a church social provided not only physical but also psychological relief. But the nexus can sometimes be a negative one (see Gottlieb (ed.), 1981, p.52), as where relatives disagree about who is to provide what (if any) help.

Thirdly, it is arguable that as well as general or local cultural 'rules' there are also family or network 'rules' legitimating and enforcing the caring and tending roles: this, indeed is a familiar point, especially since Bott's (1971) work. The converse of this is well illustrated in chapter 4, in relation to a woman's refusal to care for an elderly relative who had just returned from Australia, on the grounds that the woman had closer relatives in Belfast. Where the network is deficient, or not active, such 'rules' are less likely to be enforced.

Fourthly, the care provided by statutory services is particularly relevant to the defendedness of those who lack close caring kin and/or active networks. The members of the first group of severely disabled, who are mainly dependent on statutory carers, discussed above, are all seen as 'defended'. Possibly with the gradual reduction of home help hours and other services this will be less true. A few cases have, however, been noted where statutory services could effectively have supplemented informal care - for example, the case of Morrison, a son caring for his elderly and disabled mother (see chapter 9). Some complaints were made of tardy, inadequate or refused help by social services (for example, by Mrs Thompson) but where services were provided they seemed generally to be effective (see chapter 5 for further discussion).

Alongside the points we have made mainly in connection with care given by kin it must be noted that a part, if a lesser one, is played by neighbours. We illustrate this by looking at neighbourhood relations at the level of one particular 'close' which contains a majority of elderly and disabled.

Springdale consists of eight semi-detached cottages in a small partly-grassed close, and another four facing the road out of which the close leads. Each house has a small garden. The houses were designed for elderly couples or single people, though some of the tenants are below retiring age. All eight of the households in the close and three of the others were interviewed. Ten of the eleven households contained one or more elderly persons, but in one there was also a young married couple with a child living with the wife's pensioner mother. Five were one-person households. Half the people had lived in the close at least ten years, and all but one over five years, so one might expect social relationships to be well established. There was a range of social class levels, from quite affluent middle class (well off ex-farmers) to, for example, a former domestic servant, with a low income. All but one of the eleven households contained a disabled person, but the activities of only two were severely limited by their disability. Three people received home help services, one three or four visits per day.

The young family living with a pensioner mother were not interviewed, but among the other eleven families four had quite extensive and effective kin networks outside Springdale, three medium, two limited. Two more were isolated (with no contact with kin in the last month). As might be expected adult offspring figured much more prominently as a source of social contacts than did siblings. Social contacts with non-kin outside Springdale appeared approximately to reflect that with kin (full information was not available). Most of the people in Springdale did not own cars.

It follows that for nearly half of the families an appreciable part of their social contacts - hence informal help - would have to be found in Springdale. However Springdale made an appreciable social contribution even in the lives of those with outside friends or relatives.

The main social relationships in Springdale appear to have been those indicated by arrows in the diagram below [1] (the numbers are case numbers. Arrows with two heads indicate broadly reciprocal interaction, those with one one-way).

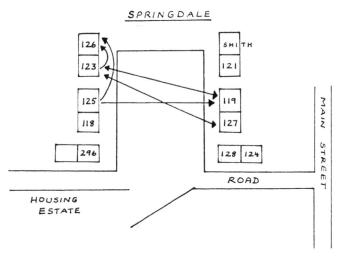

[1] Some alterations have been made in the interests of confidentiality.

Mr Smith is an elderly man, living on his own, who is 'simple'; he does indeed initiate interaction with several people in the close especially 124 (Peters) and 121 (the Collins) but is generally not highly regarded. He is seen as rather a ne'er-do-well and is frequently demanding small services, such as reading letters he receives (he is illiterate).

Mrs Green (118) (the pensioner with a young family, who is slightly disabled) has her garden dug by Mr Baines (125) but seems to have rather little other contact in the close. The two middle-aged spinster sisters, one of whom has had angina for 7 years (Collins, case 121) and who are the longest (21 years) in the close, also have little to do with other Springdalers. They are 'no longer on good terms' with Mrs McGregor (127) (a widow, suffering from arthritis and depression, with an unmarried daughter).

The Turnbulls (123), a well-off couple in their 70s, involved, but less so now than in the past, in various organisations (Masons, Orange Lodge and Women's Institute), are the most recent residents. They are friendly with Mrs McGregor (127), see daily Miss Meacher (119) (an elderly single woman, the former domestic servant, who suffers from a variety of ailments and can't walk far), and see a good deal of their almost chairfast neighbour Mrs Nelson (126). Mr Turnbull drops in for a chat with her and Mrs Turnbull takes cakes and scones when she has been baking.

The most important figure in the close is, however, Mr Baines, a 71 year old man, who retired from his work as a forester a few years ago after a severe illness. He is well-known as a ready helper, not only in Springdale. There he visits Mrs Nelson (126) daily, brings in her coal, locks up at night, and so on (Mrs Nelson also has a home help calling four times a day). He takes Miss Meacher (119) to the post office and the shops and to her late brother's grave at least once a week in his car, helps out with Smith's various problems, has sometimes given one or other of the Miss Collins' (121) a lift, and digs Mrs Green's (118) garden. Though most of these are relatively small items, Mr Baines is generally seen as someone who can always be approached for routine or (sometimes) emergency help. It is perhaps significant that his daughter (who lives with him) at first wished to prevent the researcher inter-viewing her father: she clearly felt he was being 'put upon' too much.

From this account of life in Springdale several points emerge: first, the substitution of neighbourly relations and small helping services for kinship links among elderly and sometimes isolated people in a small geographical area, defined by built form and type of housing use; second, the contribution of a natural helping person; third, the inter-weaving of statutory and informal welfare; and fourth, the factors - partly dependent on personality attributes and personal history - which, together with the distribution of stigma (Mr Smith) help to create isolation.

The detailed comments on caring in a wide range of contexts in chapter 5 provided insights into experiences of caring expressed in the carer's own terms. This chapter has pinpointed some of the key processes in kin and neighbourly care of the elderly and disabled. At a somewhat more abstract level some further comments can be made.

First, the importance of demographic factors. These include: (a) relatively high fertility rates (compared to urban areas in Northern Ireland - see Compton et al., 1985, p.141, Tables 3 and 4 - as well as Britain), especially as regards the older families from which the bulk of the disabled and those now elderly come; (b) the stability of the community; (c) the low rate of divorce and separation; and (d) the high proportion of unmarried men, particularly over the age of 45, and to a lesser extent unmarried women of that age group. These factors, taken together, mean that there is a considerable pool of potential carers/tenders relative to those likely to be needing care as well as a large number of relatives living within easy reach, in strong contrast to what has been claimed to be the situation in Britain (Parker, 1981). But the presence of many older ₍bachelors means a significant demand for care, now and in the future. The same is true, though to a lesser degree of older spinsters.

Secondly, socio-economic status, often referred to in the preceding discussion, is correlated not only with the ability to provide care/ tending directly as well as the contacts (by car, telephone and so on) on which such caring depends, but also with network size. In the Northern Ireland context, and in particular in Glengow, class differentials in fertility are comparatively small; and among a middle class which is relatively localised ('burgesses' as opposed to 'spiralists' in Bell's, 1968, terms), and partly based on farming, non-kin networks may well be more extensive than working class ones (Fischer, 1982; see also Eckenrode and Gore, 1981, p.60, for the finding that, in the US context, at least, educational and class levels are positively correlated with network size). At the lowest social class level, at least in the housing estates, a pattern of almost classic close-knit, highly localised kin and/or neighbour networks appears to exist, especially in Beechtree Park, Hollyberry Drive and Silverbirch Park (see chapter 2). This corresponds to the dense working class urban networks noted in British as well as American community studies (see Young and Willmott, 1962; Frankenberg, 1966; Bott, 1971; Gans, 1962). See also Warren's (1981) study of networks in 'parochial' (and other) communities.

It seems likely that middle class networks, as well as middle class individuals, are able to 'deliver' material goods and services more effectively than working class ones. They provide better access also to professional and statutory social services and to information and advice.

The lower working class networks, on the other hand, are likely to provide (in Glengow) somewhat closer links and more spontaneous, ungrudging help. Thus a sister (whose husband is slightly disabled) looked after her brother's three children each day for some weeks while he and his wife went potato-gathering. Analogous help is less likely in a middle class family. The non-kin part of networks tends to be based on proximity or shared situations (see Allan, 1979, on the differences between working and middle class friendships) rather than on shared interests, hence is vulnerable to physical absence. The lack of cars and telephones is of course also relevant. Households which have access to only medium or limited networks - meaning medium or limited in actual effectiveness - may be either working class or poor, but are on the whole older and in some way depleted.

This leads to the third point: small or ineffective networks and therefore poor emotional or practical support are often related to problematic situations or personal characteristics of those involved. It has been pointed out that the disabled in one-person households are rather more likely than either the married disabled or the fit elderly in one-person households to have moved into Glengow as a result of some traumatic event (often, but not always, death of the spouse). As suggested, physical transplanting, at least for poorer people, tends to break up networks and to make it difficult to form new ones. Examples have been given of people whose mental handicap or whose rather prickly personalities have probably reduced the size of their networks. The disabled tend to lose members from their networks, and this for obvious reasons, is true of the old.

For the sake of completeness, we should at this level record once again the importance of everyday cultural 'rules' which so strongly enjoin kinship solidarity in general, and caring for disabled or elderly kin in particular. These also define the conditions of such caring. They have been dealt with in detail in chapter 5, and also in chapters 1 and 11. And, fifthly, social services' policy, particularly as regards home helps, is clearly relevant. This too has been dealt with more fully elsewhere.

The character and extent of caring for the disabled and the elderly in Glengow is, in short, influenced by factors which are of much wider applicability, but whose particular application in a rural community probably differs considerably from that in a large town or city in Northern Ireland. There is some indirect evidence, from McCafferty (1985) and other work, that Glengow is likely to be not too unrepresentative of other places of the same size in the north of the Province, though it does have a larger middle-class element than McCafferty's villages.

11 Concluding analysis

In this final chapter we offer a summary of our main findings and make comments regarding future research, professional training and social policy. We also look at the prospects for informal welfare in Glengow. Of course, given the focus of our work, it is perhaps inevitable that we say relatively little about Northern Ireland as opposed to informal welfare. However, we would nevertheless like to think that our study will contribute to the process of understanding life in the Province; for, as Harris says (1972, p.225):

> Ulster ... provides an illustration of the fact that a real under- standing of a socially divided society, however its groups be defined, depends not only on the analysis of the political and economic structure at the top but also on an examination of the society at the grass-roots level.

Behind and indeed qualifying the varying levels of generality at which discussions of Northern Ireland are very often conducted are the experiences of ordinary people in their everyday lives. It is an aspect of these experiences which we have explored.

INFORMAL WELFARE IN GLENGOW

One of the main objectives of our study was to portray informal welfare 'from the inside' - to show something of the social meanings and 'rules' of giving and receiving help. The sociological reasons for this were described in chapter 1. Only with such an approach, alert to context, could we make a claim to understand the whos and whys and hows of informal welfare, and be able adequately to explore attitudes towards welfare professionals and also how social policy might best 'engage' with informal welfare.

We found as features of informal helping the points which follow:

1   The principal burden of care for those unable to function adequately on their own, especially when intensive and intimate physical care is involved, is borne mainly by women. This is true whether or not the carer lives in the same household as the person cared for. The distribution of caring tasks between women and men tends closely to follow the traditional sexual division of labour which operates in the nuclear family.

2   When care is required the task usually falls primarily to <u>one</u> member of the family. In order of preference, for adults, this member is generally (as available):

(a) a spouse

(b) an unmarried child, preferably a daughter but, if need be, a son

(c) a married daughter

(d) a married daughter-in-law

(e) some other female relative.

3   When a man is caring for his wife more help is received from family, neighbours and friends - and statutory agencies - than when a woman is caring for her husband.

4   Since the obligation to care is seen as inherent in the kinship relationship, if to varying degrees (see 2 above), and since such obligations are reinforced by social services, closely-related carers (spouses, parents, children and to a lesser extent siblings) effectively have no choice but to care for their dependent relatives, especially those in the same household. Few people actively <u>choose</u> to care, in the sense of long-term or/and high-commitment, primary as opposed to short-term or low-commitment, secondary care. As Parker (1981) and Wills (1982) point out, tending itself in time may establish or increase both affection <u>and</u> a sense of obligation.

5   In response to questions on probable source of help when ill or comfort when 'feeling down' it appeared that help was more likely to be sought from relatives than from neighbours or friends. This is in line with other studies such as Wenger, 1984, and Black et al., 1983. However, people in Glengow were more likely to seek help from the extended family <u>outside</u> of the household than in these other studies. Wenger (ibid.) found that more than half of respondents would seek help within the household but only one in six would from relatives outside it. In Glengow only three-tenths would seek help from within the nuclear family whereas more than a third (38 out of 103) would seek help from outside relatives. This implies stronger kinship ties in Glengow than in Wenger's North Wales.

6   Kin were of prime importance, not only in tending and, as the previous point suggests, in giving emotional support, but in the provision of sometimes considerable material help or assistance (for example in building or cleaning a house), information (for example about job vacancies) and advice.

7   When kin were available neighbours seldom provided sustained
     personal care.   They did render small services such as
     baby-sitting, passing on information and giving support such as a
     social chat. About a third of respondents (see 5 above) mentioned
     neighbours and friends as people they would turn to if feeling
     down.   When kin were not available they at least partially took
     over their functions (compare Hunt, 1978) but only exceptionally
     became responsible for intimate, personal care.

8   Neighbours often seemed to be waiting to be asked to give
     assistance by those caring for someone, and, paradoxically, carers
     often seemed to be waiting for help to be offered.

9   Demanding and sustained caring often brings isolation and what is
     felt to be a 'narrow' life.   However, satisfactions were often
     expressed in moving terms and were clearly of great importance to
     the carers.

10   There was often an initial wariness expressed by parents of
     disabled children over sending their child to the special care
     ·school (despite subsequent satisfaction with all aspects of the
     school). This may have been due to a tendency to avoid acknow-
     ledging that their child was not 'normal' and that he or she needed
     special care.   There were two cases where parents had initially
     sent their mentally subnormal child to the local school rather than
     to the special care school.

11   Disabled children received little care from outside the household.
     Help from neighbours, whether or not offers of help were actually
     made, was viewed in the light of two informal 'rules' by parents:
     that the responsibility placed on the neighbour would be too great;
     and that the special needs and nature of the disabled child could
     not be properly understood by a neighbour. This may also relate in
     some instances to the experience of stigma (see Philip and
     Duckworth, 1982) and to the construction of 'theodicies' (Voysey,
     1975) which emphasise the separate world of the disabled, and also
     to the inability on the part of parents to reciprocate such
     kindness.

12   Although there were exceptions, the clergy seemed in general
     peripherally rather than centrally involved in informal welfare.
     This was surprising, given the prominent place occupied by the
     churches in Northern Ireland. However, such support as was given
     was greatly valued.

13   Size of effective networks and successful functioning of both
     cared-for and carer ('defendedness') are related.   Although this
     finding rests on very small numbers it of course relates to
     previous conclusions on the importance of social support for health
     (for a good discussion see Hays and Di Matteo, 1981, esp. pp.122-
     130).   The factors which appear to underlie this relationship
     include the somewhat greater caring resources available in a larger
     network – even though the main burden of personal care tends to
     fall on one person – and also the presence of psychological support
     for the principal carer, whether this comes from husband, children,
     friends or siblings.

14   McCafferty's (1985) finding of an appreciably higher level of
      contact between Catholic informants and their relatives - in her
      view this is related to the Catholic religious teaching on the
      family - is not borne out by this study, even though the relatives
      of Catholic informants lived closer to them than did those of
      Protestants. This finding, of course, says nothing about the
      quality of interaction between family members, or the amount of
      informal helping.

To these points we wish to add some comments on relationships between
formal and informal welfare.

We found little in the way of major 'deviant' definitions of 'good
outcomes' among the people studied in Glengow. Nobody quite produced
the memorable comment of one participant in the study by Young and
Willmott (1962, p.53): 'I take more notice of my mum than I do of the
welfare'. However, a main conclusion at which we arrive is that carers
want help from formal services (especially social work) on their own
terms. They want support at the time at which they request it, and
without being patronised. Useful information and help from
professionals was welcomed in general. Carers seemed essentially to
want to get on with tasks in their own way, exemplified by the
respondent who said that she was 'not interested in social workers
coming round to my house unless there is a special reason'. Also
expressed was a sense of powerlessness in the face of statutory
agencies.

As reported earlier, relatively few people had a clear idea of the
main tasks performed by social workers. It should be remembered,
though, that social workers were not very accessible to people in
Glengow. They were based some distance away and others such as the
police and general practitioners often undertook what would otherwise
have been some of their tasks.

Home helps emerged from our study as straddling the line between
formal and informal welfare. They usually work in their local area and
typically have known their clients before working as a home help: thus
it is not surprising that nearly all of the home helps who were
interviewed claimed that help was given beyond the time allocated and
for which pay was given. But their ambivalent position in this respect
was reflected in a view expressed about them which was critical: what
they were doing was really ordinary neighbourliness and for this they
should not be paid.

Finally, in this section, we offer some more general observations
about the social make-up of Glengow.

Glengow appears as a stable community, lacking pressures for rapid
change such as a tourist trade (see Blacking et al., 1978; and
McCafferty, 1985). Population is growing only slowly. One large town
and three smaller ones are within a radius of fifteen miles, but Glengow
retains a distinct identity. A large part of the social and
recreational life of its people takes place within Glengow.

Over one-third of close relatives live in or within five miles of
Glengow and nearly three-quarters live within twenty miles. These
features are clearly important for the strength of kin and neighbour
ties, and the informal helping dependent upon them.

Contact with kin is frequent: four-fifths of the parents and nearly two-thirds of adult offspring of informants had been seen within the previous week. The nuclear family is a strong unit, given the available indices of breakdown, such as single parenthood and divorce. Traditional sex roles are often followed. However, among just over half of married couples both husband and wife are employed, a figure not much different to that for the United Kingdom as a whole.

Social class affiliation is important in relation to informal welfare and, more generally, in ability to 'cope' with life's problems. The middle class and to a slightly lesser extent the upper working class, as defined in chapter 2, benefit from a number of substantial advantages. In particular, their material resources, or access to such (for example, credit) helps them to weather crises. Their social networks, which are relatively loose and extensive (Granovetter, 1973), enable them to tap both material resources, expertise and 'influence'. They themselves are more likely than lower working class people to have leadership positions, for instance in voluntary organisations, and they tend to have the sophistication and self-confidence to make the best use of the social services. Finally, as the Black Report (1980) and other studies have documented, there is a marked class differential in both morbidity and mortality in favour of the middle and upper classes.

The 'poor' (Class 4), on the other hand, face problems of low income, high unemployment and high morbidity. However, their networks, though readily disrupted by distance and various calamities, nevertheless through their highly-localised and close-knit texture provide solid and generous emotional support.

MATTERS ARISING

Our research leads us to make comments on three fronts: further research; professional training; social policy.

Further research

There was a large 'pilot study' aspect to our research. We wanted to view informal welfare as a whole (other studies had tended to look at particular 'client groups') and to tap the contexts of helping (other studies had not, certainly when the research began, paid much attention to this). So, although we believe we have produced important substantive findings, we identify areas where more research is needed.

In doing so we are keeping three things in mind; that research into informal welfare is now expanding - it is therefore not possible for us to know of all the studies underway; that there are 'pure' as well as policy-related reasons for additional research into informal welfare - as indicated in the first chapter, notice of it needs to be taken in 'theoretical' attempts to discuss welfare matters; and that further studies of informal welfare can throw much light on a current set of concerns about 'service delivery' in particular. The last point can be amplified by reference to Smith (1986). Smith identifies a family of concerns which need research - they all affect the quantity and quality of services received by patients and clients of formal agencies. They are: the ideologies and impacts of front-line workers in service delivery; the role and impact of user perspectives on service delivery;

the importance of inter-organisational relations and the overall system of care; and the impact of organisational structures upon service delivery. These topics, Smith says, have already been studied, but not sufficiently; and they are clearly 'policy relevant', they are inter-related, they have theoretical potential, they are about managing contraction (in times of economic adversity), and they link with other topics to do with the future of welfare. They are thus 'good' topics for research. With the exception <u>perhaps</u> of Smith's topic 'the impact of organisational structures upon service delivery' his list of research priorities can profitably be pursued in each of the areas for research which we now list. As suggested above the <u>directly</u> policy-orientated emphasis of the projects varies.

<u>Rules of informal helping</u> - Systematic explorations are required into the practical reasoning involved in informal helping (including their social and cultural 'groundings'), such as <u>who</u> should help and <u>how</u> best to help someone, and of the rules implicit in decisions about when to help and when not (see, for example the eighth point made above). A full 'sociology of morals' in the field of informal welfare is needed to improve the quality of academic analyses of welfare matters, and also to assist in the evaluation of proposals for relating social work and informal welfare more closely, such as contained in the Barclay Report (1982).

<u>Isolates and isolated carers</u> - From time to time we have mentioned people who appeared to belong to no networks, to have no informal help. We feel that research is required to examine how and why people become isolated and hence receive no help from kin or neighbours. The isolation of carers too needs fuller study. Relatively little systematic analysis of the isolated who are not disabled or elderly has been carried out - though there is some evidence of newcomers being so after, for example, bereavement (compare Wenger's comments on the English retirement residents in North Wales, 1981). Our analysis of the over 60s and the disabled clearly demonstrates that those who are isolated or/and 'defeated' tend to be:

(a) those with relatively small effective networks;

(b) poor;

(c) those who have recently come from outside Glengow (district) - usually late in life;

(d) those who have recently suffered a crisis in their lives which involved a change in life pattern (for example, not only bereavement but having to move to live with a daughter).

<u>Relationships between formal and informal welfare which affect pregnant</u> <u>women and mothers of children at a young age</u> - We have noted in chapter 1 that the elderly and handicapped (including children) receiving care at home have been reasonably extensively studied. But the range of informal advice and help given to women (and men) in the relatively 'routine' situations of pregnancy and bringing up young children has not been similarly explored. We need to know about the advice and help coming from kin, neighbours and friends and the extent to which it acts as a 'filter' when contact is made with professionals. As well as yielding new knowledge about informal welfare in the context of

'everyday' conditions such studies would probably help answer pressing questions about geographical and social class variations in the 'take-up' of relevant formal services and the attention paid to the advice given, and variations in infant mortality rates (see Roberts, 1981; Smith, 1986; and Whittaker, 1986).

Comparative studies - The previous research areas should ideally be pursued with comparative dimensions. But comparative studies of all aspects of informal welfare should be a high priority. We need to know what aspects of informal welfare relate to whether a community is, for example, urban or rural, or new or old. Such studies should be undertaken from a sociological point of view. It would be most desirable too to discover what the formal/informal 'mix' is in other countries. One may presume that any country, not only the United Kingdom (with its differing regional circumstances and legislation) may find ways forward for its social policy by a knowledge of the experience of other countries. The Republic of Ireland, France, the Netherlands and West Germany seem particularly appropriate comparisons in the United Kingdom context.

Home helps - Home helps have emerged as of particular interest. They are part of both formal and informal welfare. Further studies could well yield useful insights into why people become paid carers, and also indicate the potential they have for assisting informal helpers.

Professional training

It is our impression that there is a need for more attention to be paid to a sensitive understanding of informal welfare at all the levels of training directed at social workers. A particular focus should be placed on the context in which home helps work. If it is possible for they themselves to receive some training in this respect this would prove advantageous, we believe. There should be a co-ordinated effort towards meeting such ends, with government and voluntary and educational bodies participating.

Social policy

Our study accords with other work in showing that female carers receive less help than males from statutory agencies. At the levels of both legislation and agency practice it is important that any stereotyping of sex-roles should be questioned, and that, in particular, more account should be taken of the precise circumstances and aspirations of each and every carer, male or female.

We also find merit in a number of the proposals of the Equal Opportunities Commission document Who Cares for the Carers? (1982b). Thus making available free of charge to carers essential household appliances which would make their tasks easier deserves further consideration, as does time off from work (with pay) for carers in certain circumstances. But there is a risk, as with the proposal for a non-taxable non- contributory 'Carer's Benefit', that informal welfare could end up 'colonised' and, indeed, threatened. For, presumably, money and time would have to be used 'properly'.

The encouragement of short-term admission to residential care for the elderly as well as short-term respite care ('foster a granny'), already under way on a small scale in Northern Ireland (in the Eastern and

Northern Boards) as well as in various English authorities, is desirable. An extension of the 'Cross-roads' or similar schemes could provide invaluable aid to hard-pressed carers. However, such developments need to be undertaken with the circumstances and wishes of both carers and cared-for clearly established. In this connection we draw attention to paragraph 31 of the Report of the Social Services Committee of the House of Commons on Community Care (the focus of the Report is mental illness and handicap). The Committee records difficulties in identifying the authentic voice of the ultimate consumers of community care. However, whilst there are sometimes practical problems of communication these are not insuperable. So the Committee urges a major change in the way in which services operate:

> Services are still mainly designed by providers and not users, whether families or clients, and in response to blueprints rather than in answer to demand. Matching the service to the consumer rather than vice versa should be one central aim of community care in the future. We recommend that all agencies responsible ensure that plans for services are devised with as well as for mentally disabled people and their families.

Our study does _not_ lead us to see significant scope for making informal help into a _substitute_ for statutory or voluntary agency provision, although these agencies can act as valuable and valued _supporters_ of informal help. We did find evidence of carers living tightly circumscribed lives, lonely and isolated, and often 'at their limit'. There were, though, no examples of either this or the 'non-professional' nature of the care leaving the cared-for person notably disadvantaged. Social workers do need to take account of informal carers and resources. However, this is _not_ to recommend a substitute form of caring (informal as opposed to formal) but something we regard as a rather neglected essential of good social work practice when dealing with clients. More particularly, we believe that social workers should consider the experience and points of view of carers very seriously when working with them. (As argued in chapter 8 the use of informal networks as channels of information on welfare and other benefits is likely to assist those in need without 'colonising' - see Abrams, 1980 - the networks).

Our experience of Glengow thus leaves us doubtful about whether social workers can somehow significantly increase the amount of informal help. The 'rules' which we found in neighbouring would be a particular barrier. Insensitive attempts to 'direct' informal help could lead to resentment and perhaps damage to it. Again, we feel it useful to refer to the Social Services Committee Report. It notes that care often involves arduous and unremitting work, becoming more so as carers and cared-for get older (a demographic fact), and that such care falls on women (mothers) with little support from friends, neighbours or even extended family. So they recommend, to make the costs of policy initiatives quite explicit, 'that all community care plans provide a statement of their impact on families caring for mentally disabled relatives and specify the actions to be taken in consequence' (para. 168).

There is probably scope for an increase in voluntary work, especially of the self-help category. Reference has been made in chapter 8 to parents' groups for handicapped children and a toy library, which, however, seem to be rather poorly supported. There is probably a latent demand in Glengow and elsewhere for these and other types of self-help activity, which might, as Abrams (ibid.) argues, in themselves contribute to what he calls 'the new neighbourhoodism', that is, informal relation-ships that spring from co-operation in a common venture rather than geographical contiguity. A petition for better services drawn up some years ago by the people of Ballyreagh is an apparently isolated example of 'grass roots' action.

The Barclay Report (1982) is probably the most recent important document so far as policy is concerned on the relationship between informal welfare and statutory provision. We thus wish explicitly to consider some of our findings in the light of some of its conclusions. Our findings emphasise the statement that to undertake social care planning 'social workers require knowledge of the relevant local communities and communities of interest' (ibid., p.51). We have in particular drawn attention to the need to consider the 'rules' which govern the help given and by and to whom. We also found that clients and potential clients of social workers expressed a definite view of what they wanted and expected. An awareness of this should be helpful to social workers. We thus confirm the conclusion in the Report that clients 'look for a direct, and most often a practical response, to problems and expect social workers to have knowledge, including specialist knowledge, enabling them to provide it' (ibid., p.176). However, our work does not suggest that the encouraging by social workers of informal care would lead to less of a need for other kinds of social work. We thus have reservations about the claim that 'if social work were directed at their (i.e. informal carers) support it is likely that the need for formal services to take over would be reduced' (ibid., p.217). We do, however, believe that sensitive, close co-operation between social workers and informal helpers can serve to meet need more swiftly and more effectively, through better communication in both directions between social workers and their clients, through earlier and more accurate identification of problems and through readier access to professional help. There is evidence that such benefits have flowed from adoption of a 'community-orientated' approach (see the Barclay Report conclusions on p.217; and Hadley and McGrath, 1984, and Bayley et al., 1984). The elements of such an approach do already exist - we have cited the 'bridging' function of home helps - but need to be strengthened.

In concluding this section we should like to emphasise that informal welfare, even voluntary social work, is not merely not a substitute for but essentially presupposes a solid base of material provision and services (aids, adaptations, home helps, etc.) and, where appropriate, professional skills. It is an invaluable resource, but one not to be taken for granted, now or in the future.

THE PROSPECTS FOR INFORMAL WELFARE IN GLENGOW

The future of informal welfare in Glengow must surely follow upon change (or stability) in the social milieu and cultural values which now underpin them. If, as seems likely, these follow a path similar to those in the Province and the United Kingdom as a whole, then the following observations apply. First, current 'favourable' 'demographic' factors will steadily give way to 'unfavourable' ones, with smaller families, and hence smaller kin networks supporting a larger proportion of disabled elderly. Second, economic conditions in the area are likely to deteriorate further, increasing the stresses brought by unemployment and poverty. But this will possibly not, given a relatively prosperous farming industry, be a very severe deterioration. Third, kinship values are likely to change in the direction of those current in urban situations. This will, on present indications, be a gradual process, though accelerated by the subject of the first point above. The apparently minimal changes in conjugal role segregation noted by McCafferty (1985) as compared with Young and Willmott's 'symmetrical family' (1973) underscores the slowness of change in kinship values. Fourth, government policy, in relation to statutory services and benefit provision (and to the private market in welfare) may change. It seems possible that statutory services will be further curtailed and, if so, that informal welfare help which has striven so hard to maintain a rather fragile equilibrium between success and failure, will often be unable to prevent a serious deterioration in overall standards of care.

Our study indicates that informal welfare is a most valuable complement to statutory services. One of the aims of policy should be, cautiously and sensitively, to strengthen and extend it but it can in no circumstances be seen as an alternative to such services, nor can the latter safely be withdrawn in favour of the former.

APPENDICES

INFORMAL WELFARE PROJECT

QUESTIONNAIRE 1

Name of Respondent ....

Address ....

Domestic status of respondent ....

Household Composition

Domestic status or relation to respondent	Marital Status	Name	Age	Occupation	Employment	Code
Respondent						

5. <u>Kin (Outside Household)</u>

	Name	Marital Status	Age	Address	When last contacted	Where last contacted	No. of times contacted last seven days	Coding
a) Respondents	M							
	F							
	B/Z1							
	2							
	3							
	4							
	5							
	6							
	7							
	8							
b) Respondent or a)'s H or other (specify)	M							
	F							
	B/Z1							
	2							
	3							
	4							
	5							
	6							
	7							
	8							
c) Children living outside Household	1							
	2							
	3							
	4							
	5							
	6							

6. Contact with any of the following during last 30 days

	At Subjects Home			Elsewhere			Contact by Telephone			Coding
	Female Respondent	Male Respondent or Spouse	Other (Specify)	Female Respondent	Male Respondent or Spouse	Other	Female Respondent	Male Respondent or Spouse	Other	
G.P.										
Nurse										
Physiotherapist/ Speech therapist										
Health Visitor										
Social Worker/ Asst.										
Home Help										
S.S. Official										
Housing Executive										
Police										
Teacher										
Clergyman										
Insurance Agent										
Other										

123

7. Is any member of the household or the family chronically sick, physically handicapped, mentally handicapped or mentally ill?

In household:	Nature of Handicap	Degree of Handicap	Registered Disabled?	Coding
Who?				
....				
Any Others				
....				
....				
....				
In Family				
Who?				
....				
Any Others				
....				
....				

Comments

Date ....

Time ....

Name ....

124

APPENDIX B

1. Name:

2. Address:

3. How long have you lived at this address?

4. How long have you lived in Glengow?

5. Where did you grow up?

6. Does anyone in the household have a car?

7. Do you have a telephone?

8. Household Composition:

Domestic status or relation to respondent	Marital Status	Name	D.O.B.	Present or last occup.	Employment Status
Respondent					

Questionnaire No.

9. Family (outside the household)

	Name	Marital Status	D.O.B. or Age	Address	When last contacted by Phone	Letter	In person	Where	Present or last Occup.	Employ ment Status	No of personal contact within last 30 days
a) Woman's family											
Mother											
Father											
Brothers and Sisters 1											
2											
3											
4											
5											
6											
7											
8											
b) Man's Family											
Mother											
Father											
Brothers and Sisters 1											
2											
3											
4											
5											
7											
8											
c) Children living outside household 1											
2											
3											
4											
5											

126

10. Is there any member of the family chronically sick or handicapped in any way?

a) <u>In household</u>   Nature and Severity of
                                          Handicap. _____

   Who? _____

   _____

   _____

b) <u>In Family</u> (outside of the house-
                    hold)

   Who? _____

   _____

   _____

   If answer to Question 10 is <u>yes</u> move to Question 11
   If answer to Question 10 is <u>no</u> move to Question 12

11. Who is mainly responsible for the care of _____?
    (person(s) named in 10a or 10b). Is any help received from the
    social services?

Name of Carer	Name of Person Cared for	Help from Social Services
_____	_____	_____
_____	_____	_____
_____	_____	_____
_____	_____	_____
_____	_____	_____

Comments (if volunteered)

12. Is anyone in the household involved in caring for anybody else?

Name of Carer	Name of Person Cared For	Relation between the two — are they friends relatives etc?
_____	_____	_____
_____	_____	_____
_____	_____	_____

If answer to question 12 is <u>Yes</u> move to question 13.
If answer to question 12 is <u>No</u> move to question 15.

13. (Ask only if somebody <u>within the household</u> is caring for someone).

a) What form does this care take?

Prompt if necessary with:
    i) shopping
   ii) cooking
  iii) cleaning (of house)
  iv) washing (of clothes)
   v) washing (of person)
  vi) bathing
 vii) feeding
viii) toileting
  ix) dressing
   x) keeping him/her company

1st person named:

2nd person named:

b) For each task mentioned ask how frequently or how much time is spent per day/per week by the carer.

TASK	Times per day	Times per week	Hours per week
i shopping			
ii cooking			
iii cleaning			
iv washing			
v washing			
vi bathing			
vii feeding			
viii toileting			
ix dressing			
x keeping him/her company			

<u>Comments</u>: (if volunteered)

14. Ask only if respondent is a carer, otherwise move to question 15.

    a) What are the main difficulties involved in caring for

       1st person named? :

       2nd person named? :

    b) Is there anything that you can think of which would improve your situation, or situation of (name of person cared for)?

    c) Would the following be of any help? Please say if you have already made use of any of:

	Would be of Use	Already Used
i) Short stay residential care for (name) to let you have a break		
ii) day centre		
iii) a nurse coming into the home to help during the day		
iv) a nurse coming into the home to help during the night		
v) meeting other people in the same situation as yourself		
vi) financial help		

(Please indicate if these situations apply to more than one person).

15. Who would you turn to for help in the following situations?:

    a) If you were ill and could not leave the house and needed shopping done:-

    b) If you were feeling down and just wanted somebody to talk to:-

16. Are there any sorts of people from whom you would be unwilling to receive help yourself?

    (Prompt if necessary) - If for example you were unwell,

    (Prompt if necessary) -

    a) Newcomers to the area or people you don't know very well

    b) People of a different religion to yourself

    c) People who are much richer or much poorer than you

    d) People who are very different from you

    e) Somebody from social services

17. Are there any sorts of people that you would be unwilling to help for any reason?

    (Prompt if necessary as above (Q.16) except for (e)).

18. I am going to read out 2 examples of people who are in difficulty and I would like your opinion.

    a) Imagine you know a family where the father has been off work for some time and living on sick pay. They are in trouble making the money go round and are getting behind with the electricity. Where do you think they should go for help?

    b) Suppose an old couple live next door to you and for a few months you have been getting worried about them. Their home is badly in need of decoration and their health is failing. You know that they are too independent to ask for help and yet they seem to need it. Who do you think should help them?

Name of interviewer:

Date:

APPENDIX C

1. Name:

2. Address:

3. How long have you lived at this address?

4. How long have you lived in Glengow?

5. Where did you grow up?

6. Does anyone in the household have a car?

7. Do you have a telephone?

8. Household Composition:

Domestic status or relation to respondent	Marital Status	Name	D.O.B.	Present or last occup.	Employment Status
Respondent					

131

9. Family (outside the household)

	Name	Marital Status	D.O.B. or Age	Address	When last contacted by				Present or last Occup.	Employ ment Status	No of personal contact within last 30 days
					Phone	Letter	In person	Where			
a) Woman's family											
Mother											
Father											
Brothers and Sisters 1											
2											
3											
4											
5											
6											
7											
8											
b) Man's Family											
Mother											
Father											
Brothers and Sisters 1											
2											
3											
4											
5											
7											
8											
c) Children living outside household 1											
2											
3											
4											
5											

132

10. Is there any member of the family chronically sick or handicapped in any way?

a) In household   Nature and Severity of Handicap. _____

    Who? _____

    _____

    _____

b) In Family (outside of the house-
             hold)

    Who? _____

    _____

    _____

If answer to Question 10 is yes move to Question 11
If answer to Question 10 is no move to Question 12

11. Who is mainly responsible for the care of _____?
(person(s) named in 10a or 10b). Is any help received from the social services?

Name of Carer	Name of Person Cared for	Help from Social Services
_____	_____	_____
_____	_____	_____
_____	_____	_____
_____	_____	_____
_____	_____	_____

Comments (if volunteered)

12. Is anyone in the household involved in caring for anybody else?

Name of Carer	Name of Person Cared For	Relation between the two - are they friends relatives etc?

If answer to question 12 is Yes move to question 13.
If answer to question 12 is No move to question 15.

13. (Ask only if somebody within the household is caring for someone).

   a) What form does this care take?

   Prompt if necessary with:
   - i) shopping
   - ii) cooking
   - iii) cleaning (of house)
   - iv) washing (of clothes)
   - v) washing (of person)
   - vi) bathing
   - vii) feeding
   - viii) toileting
   - ix) dressing
   - x) keeping him/her company

1st person named:

2nd person named:

   b) For each task mentioned ask how frequently or how much time is spent per day/per week by the carer.

TASK	Times per day	Times per week	Hours per week
i shopping			
ii cooking			
iii cleaning			
iv washing			
v washing			
vi bathing			
vii feeding			
viii toileting			
ix dressing			
x keeping him/her company			

Comments: (if volunteered)

14. Ask only if respondent is a carer, otherwise move to question 15.

    a) What are the main difficulties involved in caring for

        1st person named? :

        2nd person named? :

    b) Is there anything that you can think of which would improve your situation, or situation of (name of person cared for)?

    c) Would the following be of any help? Please say if you have already made use of any of:

	Would be of Use	Already Used
i) Short stay residential care for (name) to let you have a break		
ii) day centre		
iii) a nurse coming into the home to help during the day		
iv) a nurse coming into the home to help during the night		
v) meeting other people in the same situation as yourself		
vi) financial help		

(Please indicate if these situations apply to more than one person).

15. Who would you turn to for help in the following situations?:

    a) If you were ill and could not leave the house and needed shopping done:-

    b) If you were feeling down and just wanted somebody to talk to:-

16. Are there any sorts of people from whom you would be unwilling to receive help yourself?

    (Prompt if necessary) - If for example you were unwell,

    (Prompt if necessary) -

    a) Newcomers to the area or people you don't know very well

    b) People of a different religion to yourself

    c) People who are much richer or much poorer than you

    d) People who are very different from you

    d) Somebody from social services

17. Are there any sorts of people that you would be unwilling to help for any reason?

    (Prompt if necessary as above (question 16 except for (e)).

18. What do you consider the main tasks of social workers to be?

Name of interviewer:

Date:

APPENDIX D

INDEX OF CONTACTS

Most recent

Contact	Telephone	Letter	Personal	Score
10 yrs or over ago	Any one or comb of these			0
5 and under	–	√	–	½
10	√	– √	–	½
years	–√	– √	√	1
2 and under	–	√	–	1
5	√	– √	–	1
years	–√	– √	√	2
1 and under	–	√	–	2
2	√	– √	–	2
years	–√	– √	√	4
3 months and	–	√	–	3
under	√	– √	–	3
12 months	–√	– √	√	6
1 and under	–	√	–	4
3	√	– √	–	4
months	–	– √	√	8
	√	– √	√	12
8 and under	–	√	–	6
30	√	– √	–	6
days	–	– √	√	12
	√	– √	√	16
Not today or	–	√	–	6
yesterday and less	√	– √	–	9
than 8 days	–	– √	√	18
	√	– √	√	24
Today, yesterday	–	√	–	6
	√	– √	–	12
	–	– √	√	24
	√	– √	√	32

√ = contact

– = no contact

137

Explanatory Comments

The calculation of the index is somewhat complex, but the following examples may serve to elucidate it.

The contact index for a given individual is based on a combination - but not simple addition - of relevant scores. Thus, if the informant last saw her sister three weeks ago but never has telephone or letter contact the sister's contact score will be 12, represented by a tick under 'personal' column in the category 8-30 days. However, contact by letter with the sister in the same period would not increase the sister's score, as it would be assumed that the nett value (in terms of the 'goods', for instance emotional support, or information) of the personal contact would far outweigh - and not be significantly increased by - the receipt of a letter. However, where face-to-face contact is very infrequent, as, for example, where the sister is in Canada, a letter received recently would be likely to carry as much or more weight than a personal contact some years ago, and would be taken into account in computing a score. Telephone calls, however, as a much more immediate and intimate form of contact than letters are always taken into account. Thus if the sister concerned last telephoned 10 days ago as well as visiting three weeks ago then the contact score would be 12+4 (not 6) = 16, represented by a tick in the columns for telephone and personal contact. If the last personal contact was three days ago (category 'not to-day/yesterday but less than 8 days) and the last telephone call 10 days ago then score is 18+4 (the 'additional' value represented by a telephone call in that time category) = 22. Where the last telephone contact was three months or more ago its contact value is not added to that of a personal contact during the same period. Thus if EGO has last seen his sister nine months ago and had the last telephone contact with her 6 months ago the score will remain 6.

APPENDIX E

KINSHIP

Occupation of kin

How often seen?

How often do kin members see each other?

Favourites amongst kin

Relationships with and attitudes towards in laws; for example, if a woman is friendly with her Z, is her H friendly with her Z's H?

FRIENDSHIP

What is a friend?

Whom do you regularly see for a chat?

                go out with?

                tell good and bad news to?

                cheers you up if you are feeling miserable?

                have shared interests?

                helps you out e.g. with children?

Do your friends (who) see each other independently of yourself?

How did you get to know your friends (school, work etc ...)?

Where do they live? Do you visit them at home?

Have you had friends that have moved away? Do you keep in touch?

GODPARENTS

Are you a Godparent? To whom?

Why were you chosen?

What do you do as a Godparent?

What do your Godparents call you?

Do you have Godparents?

Ditto.

FARMERS

How much land? — Arable or grazing?

How much livestock?

Market? — Buy and sell where? With whom?

Employees? Who works the land?

Mutual exchange of help?

Own or rent land?

How long had the farm?

Did he buy or inherit the farm/land?

NAMES

How do you address your father/mother/in-laws/siblings/in-laws?

What do they call you?

Do you, or any of your family have nicknames?

What are they? How did they come about?

Were you named for anyone? Who? Ditto your parents/
siblings/children?

Who do you address with Mr and Mrs?

with Christian names?

LEISURE

What do you do in your spare time?

With whom? (E or group of kin or friends)

How often? Where? Clubs?

How long have you belonged to this club?

CRISES

Have any of these events taken place recently within the family:

Birth?

Marriage?

Death?

Accident?

Unemployment?

What happened?

Who was there? (e.g. at wedding)

Who helped out?

Were you surprised by the help that you got?

Were you surprised by the help that e.g. Mrs ... gave?

Why?

(PAST)

How do you think that e.g. your mother would have been helped out in a similar situation in the past?

How do you think that neighbours would have helped out in a similar situation in the past?

SEXUAL DIVISION OF LABOUR

In your family who does the : Cooking? ... always?

Washing up?

Washing?

Ironing?

Changing the baby?

Bathing the baby?

Put the children to bed?

Read story to children?

Take children on trips?

Clean windows?

Mow the lawn?

Do the shopping?

Clean the car?

Mend a fuse?

Change lightbulbs/plugs?

Lights and cleans the fire?

FARMS - Is there work that men do, and work that women do? What work? What happens if a man does women's work and v.v.? Might this happen during times of illness?

SHOP OR OTHER BUSINESS - Who does what? e.g. ordering

accounts

till?

MARRIAGE AND COURTSHIP

Where did you meet your spouse?

Did you already know her/him?

Where did you go?/What did you do when you were courting?

At what point did you meet each other's family?

How did you address your girl/boy friend's parents? - And how do you address them now and v.v.?

How long after you met/started courting did you get married?

Did you get engaged first? - How was that celebrated? (ring? party?)

Where did you get married? (Whose church?)

What happened after the wedding? e.g. reception? where?

Who was invited to the wedding/reception? (Who was not invited?)

Honeymoon?

Where did you first live after marriage?

SOCIAL SERVICES

Have you (or a member of your family) ever been unemployed?

When? What was the situation? (e.g. laid off???)

Did you receive unemployment benefit? Was it adequate?

Did you receive other state benefits? Were they adequate?

How long were you u/e for?

How did you feel about being u/e?

Have you ever had any contact with social workers? When? Why?

Were they helpful? In what way? Why not?

Have you known other people who had contact with social workers? Ditto ...

How do you think that social workers can best help people when they are in a difficult situation?

Do you think that they sometimes interfere when they are not wanted?

Do you know about home helps?

Do you think that they are a good idea, or do you think that neighbours should just help one another, especially old people, anyway?

Has the welfare state affected community life in Glengow at all? In what way?

HISTORY

What was your first job? Where?

How old were you?

Unions? Office bearer?

Hiring Fairs?

Unemployed - How did people manage in those days?

-- emigration?

Workhouses

Health

Family remedies?

Dispensary doctors?

Childbirth - midwives, handy women?

T.B.?

Kin/Friends/Neighbours

What kin (..) did you have as a child?

How much contact? Friendly? (Black sheep?)

How long had families known each other? (Neighbours?)

Friendly with kin/friends/neighbour of opposite sex?

Events

1st World War, 2nd World War, Civil War

Riots, Glengow Tragedy

Other .. (use photos)

Pilgrimages

Have you ever been to Lourdes/Knock/other pilgrimage centre?

When, who with, what for, who paid?

Do you know of any one who has been on a pilgrimage? Ditto ...

ORANGE LODGE/A.O.H.

Are you an office bearer?

How long have you been a member?

What made you join?

Was your father a member? Or B. or other kin, or friends?

Where do they meet?

How often?

Mutual help within lodge?

Recognition of other members?

SOCIAL STRATIFICATION

Is Glengow a very mixed town in terms of rich and poor?

Was it so in the past?

Who are the rich people – e.g. what kind of jobs do they do?

  Ditto the poor ...?

Are some people looked up to in the town more than others? What sort of person?

Do some people think that they are better than others?

Are richer areas more neighbourly or less neighbourly than poor areas?

What do you hope that your children will do when they grow up?

FAMILY QUESTIONNAIRE

NAME:

ADDRESS:

AGE:

1. What do you (or did you) call your parents? e.g. mammy, ma, etc.

   MOTHER:

   FATHER:

2. What do you (or did you) call your grandparents? e.g. granny, granma, etc.

   MOTHER'S MOTHER:

   MOTHER'S FATHER:

   FATHER'S MOTHER:

   FATHER'S FATHER:

If you are married ...

3. How old were you when you married?

4. Where is your own home place?

   Where is your husband's home place?

5. What does your husband (or did your husband) call his parents?

   MOTHER:

   FATHER:

6. What does he (or did he) call your parents?

   MOTHER:

   FATHER:

7. What do you (or did you) call his parents?

   MOTHER:

   FATHER:

8. How did you meet your husband? e.g. through relatives, through friends, at a dance, etc.

Everybody...

9. Is there somebody in your family who keeps all the members of the family in touch with family events? (e.g. weddings, illness, etc.)

   If so who is it? e.g. yourself? your mother? etc.

Thank you very much for answering these questions.

KEEPING THE DIARY

The diary is set out in such a way as to help you record your daily activities. However if it seems too rigid, then please feel free to record the information in the way that you feel is best.

Page 1

Day and Date   Please give the day of the week and the date for each entry.

Times   Please write down the approximate time that you began each activity.

What did you do   Briefly say what you did at different times throughout the day.

People seen to
talk to   Please say who you met during the day, and indicate how you know the person, e.g., is she a relative, a friend or a neighbour?

Where seen   Did you see the person at your house, at his or her house, or at another person's house? Or did you meet somewhere else, e.g. in the street, at the shops, at the health centre?

What did you
talk about or
do together   Please say what sort of things you talked about. If you do not want to tell us then you may leave this section blank.

Comments,
feelings,
anything else?   Please mention here any letters that you sent or received and any phone calls that you made or received. Also anything else you wish to add about the day's events.

Page 2.

Meals   We are interested in what people eat and the names given to the different meals. Please fill in the time that you ate; what you normally call that meal; what you ate; who got the meal ready; and who ate it with you.

Page 3

Any extra
comments   Please tell us if you think that the day has been a typical day for you. At the end of seven days, tell us if it has been a typical week, and say why (or why not) this is so. You may put any other comments or information on this page too.

Example

As you will see, the first few pages of the diary are set out as an example to give you an indication of the sort of things that we are looking for. Please begin to fill in the diary on the first blank pages after the example. We would like to take this opportunity to thank you for agreeing to fill in the diary for us, and we hope that you will enjoy doing it.

APPENDIX H

Day

Date

Times	What did you do	People seen to talk to. How do you know them? e.g. friend, sister	Where seen	What did you talk about or do together?	Comments, feelings, anything else. Letters written or received. Phone calls made or received
MORNING					
AFTERNOON					
EVENING					
NIGHT					

151

Times	Name of Meal	What did you eat	Who prepared the meal?	Did you eat with anybody? Who?
MORNING				
AFTERNOON				
EVENING				
NIGHT				

ANY EXTRA COMMENTS

e.g. Has this been a typical day/week?

Or was it different from normal? If so in what way was it different?

Bibliography

Abrams, M. (1978), Beyond Three Score and Ten: A First Report on a Survey of the Elderly, Age Concern, London.

Abrams, P. (1977), 'Community care: some research problems and priorities', Policy and Politics, Vol.6, No.2, pp.125-51.

Abrams, P. (1978), Neighbourhood Care and Social Policy: A Research Perspective, Volunteer Centre, Berkhamsted.

Abrams, P. (1980), 'Social change, social networks and neighbourhood care', Social Work Service, February, pp.12-23.

Allan, G. (1979), A Sociology of Friendship and Kinship, Allen and Unwin, London.

Allan, G. (1983), 'Informal networks of care: issues raised by Barclay', British Journal of Social Work, Vol.13, No.4, pp.417-433.

Arensberg, C.M. and Kimball, S.T. (1968), Family and Community in Ireland, Harvard University Press, Cambridge, Mass.

Baldwin, S. (1985), The Costs of Caring, Routledge and Kegan Paul, London.

Ball, C. and Ball, M. (1982), What the Neighbours Say, Volunteer Centre, London.

Barclay Report (1982), Social Workers, their Role and Tasks, Report of a Working Party of the National Institute for Social Work, Bedford Square Press, London.

Bayley, M. (1973), <u>Mental Handicap and Community Care</u>, Routledge and Kegan Paul, London.

Bayley, M., Seyd, R., and Tennant, A. (1985), <u>The Final Report</u>, (Neighbourhood Services Project - Dinnington, Paper No.12), Department of Sociological Studies, University of Sheffield.

Bell, C. (1968), <u>Middle Class Families</u>, Routledge and Kegan Paul, London.

Bell, J. (1979), 'Hiring fairs in Ulster', <u>Ulster Folklife</u>, Vol.25, pp.67-78.

Biegel, D. and Naparstek, A. (eds.) (1982), <u>Community Support Systems and Mental Health</u>, Springer, New York.

Birrell, D. and Williamson, A. (1983), 'Northern Ireland's integrated health and personal social service structure', Ch.8 of Williamson, A. and Room, G. (eds.) (1983), <u>Health and Welfare States of Britain</u>, Heinemann, London.

Black Report (1980), <u>Inequalities in Health</u>, Townsend, P. and Davidson, N. (eds), Penguin, Harmondsworth.

Black, J. et al. (1983), <u>Social Work in Context</u>, Tavistock, London.

Blacking, J., Holy, L. and Stuchlik, M. (1978), <u>Situational Determinants of Recruitment in Four Northern Ireland Communities</u>, Report to the Social Science Research Council, London.

Blaxter, M. (1976), <u>The Meaning of Disability</u>, Heinemann, London.

Boissevain, J. (1974), <u>Friends of Friends</u>, Blackwell, Oxford.

Bott, E. (1971), <u>Family and Social Network</u>, 2nd ed., Free Press, New York.

Bradshaw, J. (1980), <u>The Family Fund</u>, Routledge and Kegan Paul, London.

Brenton, M. and Jones, C. (eds.) (1985), <u>The Year Book of Social Policy in Britain, 1984-85</u>, Routledge and Kegan Paul, London.

Briggs, A. and Oliver, J. (1985), <u>Caring: Experiences of Looking After Disabled Relatives</u>, Routledge and Kegan Paul, London.

Brown, G. and Harris, T. (1978), <u>The Social Origins of Depression: A Study of Psychiatric Disorder in Women</u>, Free Press, New York.

Buckley, A. (1982), <u>A Gentle People: A Study of a Peaceful Community in Northern Ireland</u>, Ulster Folk and Transport Museum, Cultra, Belfast.

Buckley, A. (1983), 'Neighbourliness - myth and history', <u>Oral History Journal</u>, Vol.II, No.I pp.44-51.

Bulmer, M. (1986), <u>Neighbours: The Work of Philip Abrams</u>, Cambridge University Press, Cambridge.

Bulmer, M. (ed.) (1982), *The Uses of Social Research*, Allen and Unwin, London.

Carrier, J. and Kendall, I. (1973), 'Social policy and social change: explanations of the development of social policy', *Journal of Social Policy*, Vol.2, No.3, pp.209-24.

Cecil, R., Offer, J. and St. Leger, F. (1985), *Informal Welfare in a Small Town in Northern Ireland: A Report to the Department of Health and Social Services, Northern Ireland*, University of Ulster, Coleraine.

Challis, D. (1981), 'The measurement of outcome in social care of the elderly', *Journal of Social Policy*, Vol.10, No.2, pp. 179-208.

Challis, D. and Davies, B. (1980), 'A new approach to community care of the elderly', *British Journal of Social Work*, Vol.10, No.1, pp.1-18.

Charlesworth, A. et al. (1984), *Carers and Services*, Equal Opportunities Commission, Manchester.

Cochran, M., Gunnarsson, L., Grabe, S. and Lewis, J. (1984), *The Social Support Networks of Mothers with Young Children: A Cross-National Comparison*, Department of Educational Research, University of Gothenburg.

Collins, A.H. and Pancoast, D.L. (1976), *Natural Helping Networks*, National Association of Social Workers, Washington.

Compton, P.A., Coward, J. and Davies, W. (1985), 'Family size and religious denomination in Northern Ireland', *Journal of Biosocial Science*, Vol.17, No.2, pp.137-145.

Connell, K. H. (1962), 'Peasant marriage in Ireland', *Economic History Review*, 2nd series, Vol.14, pp.502-23.

Dartington, T., Miller, E. and Gwynne, G. (1981), *A Life Together*, Tavistock, London.

Davies, B. and Knapp, M. (1981), *Old People's Homes and the Production of Welfare*, Routledge and Kegan Paul, London.

Deacon, R. and Bartley, M. (1975), 'Becoming a social worker', in Jones, H. (ed.), 1975, pp.69-86.

DHSS (1978), *A Happier Old Age*, HMSO, London.

DHSS (1984), *Supporting the Informal Carers*, HMSO, London.

Dingwall, R. (1976), *Aspects of Illness*, Martin Robertson, Oxford.

Dohrenwend, B.S. and Dohrenwend, B.P. (1974), *Stressful Life Events: Their Nature and Effects*, Wiley, New York.

Eckenrode, J. and Gore, S. (1981), 'Stressful events and social supports', Ch.2 of Gottlieb, B. (ed.), 1981.

Education Act (1981), Public General Acts - Elizabeth II, 1981, Ch.60.

Edwards, C.J.W. (1981), 'Structural underemployment on full time farms in Northern Ireland', Irish Journal of Agricultural Economics and Rural Sociology, Vol.8, pp.235-242.

E.O.C. (1980), The Experiences of Caring for Elderly and Handicapped Dependents, Equal Opportunities Commission, Manchester.

E.O.C. (1981), Behind Closed Doors, Equal Opportunities Commission, Manchester.

E.O.C. (1982a), Caring for the Elderly and Handicapped: Community Care Policies and Women's Lives, Equal Opportunities Commission, Manchester.

E.O.C. (1982b), Who Cares for the Carers?, Equal Opportunities Commission, Manchester.

Finch, J. and Groves, D. (eds.) (1983), A Labour of Love: Women, Work and Caring, Routledge and Kegan Paul, London.

Firth, R., Hubert, J. and Forge, A. (1969), Families and their Relatives, Routledge and Kegan Paul, London.

Fischer, C.S. et al. (1977), Networks and Places, Free Press, New York.

Fischer, C.S. (1982), To Dwell Among Friends, University of Chicago, Chicago.

Fox, R. (1978), The Tory Islanders, Cambridge University Press, Cambridge.

Frankenberg, R. (1966), Communities in Britain, Penguin, Harmondsworth.

Froland, C. et al. (1981), Helping Networks and Human Services, Sage Publications, Beverly Hills.

Gamarnikow, E. (ed.) (1983), The Public and the Private, Heinemann, London.

Gans, H.J. (1962), The Urban Villagers, Free Press, New York.

Gavron, H. (1966), The Captive Wife, Routledge and Kegan Paul, London.

Glampson, A., Glastonbury, B. and Fruin, D. (1977), 'Knowledge and perceptions of the social services', Journal of Social Policy, Vol.6, No.1, pp.1-16.

Glastonbury, B., Burdett, M. and Austin, R. (1973), 'Community perception and the social services', Policy and Politics, Vol.1, No.3, pp.191-211.

Glendinning, C. (1983), Unshared Care, Routledge and Kegan Paul, London.

Goffman, E. (1968a), Asylums, Penguin, Harmondsworth.

Goffman, E. (1968b), Stigma, Penguin, Harmondsworth.

Goldberg, E.M. and Hatch, S. (eds.) (1981), A New Look at the Personal Social Services, Policy Studies Institute, London.

Gottlieb, B. (ed.) (1981), Social Networks and Social Support, Sage, Beverly Hills.

Graham, H. (1983), 'Caring: a labour of love', in Finch, J. and Groves, D., A Labour of Love, Routledge and Kegan Paul, London, 1983.

Granovetter, M. (1973), 'The strength of weak ties', American Journal of Sociology, Vol.78, pp.1360-1380.

Graycar, A. (1983), 'Informal, voluntary and statutory services: the complex relationship, British Journal of Social Work, Vol.13, No.4, pp.379-393.

Hadley, R. and Hatch, S. (1981), Social Welfare and the Failure of the State, Allen and Unwin, London.

Hadley, R. and McGrath, M. (1980), Going Local, National Council of Voluntary Organizations, London.

Hadley, R. and McGrath, M. (1984), When Social Services are Local: The Normanton Experience, Allen and Unwin, London.

Hannan, D.F. and Katsiaouni, L.A. (1977), Traditional Families?, Economic and Social Research Institute, Dublin.

Harris, A. (1971), Handicapped and Impaired in Great Britain, 2 vols, HMSO, London.

Harris, R. (1961), 'The selection of leaders in Ballybeg, Northern Ireland', Sociological Review, Vol.9, pp.137-149.

Harris, R. (1972), Prejudice and Tolerance in Ulster, Manchester University Press, Manchester.

Hatch, S. (1980), 'The Wolfenden Report on voluntary organisations', in The Year Book of Social Policy in Britain 1978, edited by Brown, S., and Baldwin, S., Routledge and Kegan Paul, London, 1980.

Hays, R. and Di Matteo, M. (1981), 'Social support and serious illness', Ch.5 in Gottlieb, B. (ed.), 1981.

Hill, M. (1980), Understanding Social Policy, Basil Blackwell and Martin Robinson, Oxford.

Hirsch, B.J. (1980), 'Natural support systems and coping with major life changes', American Journal of Community Psychology, Vol.8, No.2, pp.159-171.

House of Commons, 2nd Report from the Social Services Committee (1985), Community Care Vol.1, HC 13-1, HMSO, London.

Hunt, A. (1978), The Elderly at Home, HMSO, London.

Isaacs, B., Livingstone, M. and Neville, Y. (1972), <u>Survival of the Unfittest: A Study of Geriatric Patients in Glasgow,</u> Routledge and Kegan Paul, London.

Isaacs, B. and Neville, Y. (1974), <u>The Measurement of Need in Old People</u>, Scottish Home and Health Department, Edinburgh.

Jacobs, J. (1965), <u>The Death and Life of Great American Cities</u>, Penguin, Harmondsworth.

Jones, H. (ed.) (1975), <u>Towards a New Social Work</u>, Routledge and Kegan Paul, London.

Jourard, S. (1971), <u>The Transparent Self</u>, Van Nostrand, New York.

Karn, V. (1977), <u>Retiring to the Seaside</u>, Routledge and Kegan Paul, London.

Knapp, M. (1984), <u>The Economics of Social Care</u>, Macmillan, Basingstoke and London.

Kohen, J. (1983), 'Old but not alone: informal social supports among the elderly by marital status and sex', <u>The Gerontologist,</u> Vol.23, No.1, pp.57-63.

Le Grand, J. (1982), <u>The Strategy of Equality</u>, Allen and Unwin, London.

Leaper, R. (1975), 'Subsidiarity and the welfare state', <u>Administration</u>, (Journal of the Institute of Public Administration of Ireland), Vol.23, No.4, pp.445-58.

Leat, D. (1983), <u>Getting to Know the Neighbours</u>, Policy Studies Unit, London.

Leyton, E. (1974), 'Irish friends and "friends": the nexus of friendship, kinship and class in Aughnaboy', in Leyton, E. (ed), 1974, <u>The Compact</u>, Memorial University of Newfoundland.

Lyons, F.S.L. (1973), <u>Ireland Since the Famine</u>, Fontana, London.

McCafferty, M.J. (1985), <u>Family and Kin in North Antrim and South Derry Villages - a Geographical Perspective,</u> M.Phil. thesis, University of Ulster, Coleraine.

McCoy, K. (1982), <u>Health and Social Services for the Very Old at Home</u>, DHSS (N. Ireland), Belfast.

Mackay, T.S. (1891), 'The interest of the working class in the poor law', in <u>Proceedings of the Poor Law Conference for the South East District</u>, Knight, London.

Mayer, J.E. and Timms, N. (1970), <u>The Client Speaks</u>, Routledge and Kegan Paul, London.

Mitchell, C. (ed.) (1969), <u>Social Networks in Urban Situations</u>, Manchester University Press, Manchester.

Mitchell, R. and Trickett, E. (1980), 'Task force report: social networks as mediators of social support', Community Mental Health Journal, Vol. 16, No.1, pp.27-44.

Nissel, M. and Bonnerjea, L. (1982), Family Care of the Handicapped Elderly: Who Pays? Policy Study Institute, London.

Oakley, A. (1974), Housewife, Allen Lane, London.

Offer, J. (1979), 'The informal system of social welfare', Social Service Quarterly, Vol.52, No.3, pp.81-84.

Offer, J. (1983), 'Spencer's sociology of welfare', Sociological Review, Vol.31, No.4, pp.719-752.

Offer, J. (1984), 'Informal welfare, social work, and the sociology of welfare', British Journal of Social Work, Vol.14, No.6, pp.545-555.

Offer, J. (1985a), 'On the need for a sociology of poverty: comments on the state of research on poverty in the United Kingdom', Social Science Information, Vol.24, No.2, pp.299-307.

Offer, J. (1985b), 'Social policy and informal welfare', Ch.10 of Brenton, M. and Jones, C. (eds.), 1985.

OUTSET Action on Handicap Survey in Northern Ireland (1982) (Whitehead, A., Bayer, S. and Buck, K.), A Report of a Survey of the Handicapped in the Coleraine, Moyle and Ballymoney Health and Social Services District, Outset, London.

Parad, H.J. (ed.) (1965), Crisis Intervention, Family Service Association of America, New York.

Parker, G. (1985), With Due Care and Attention, Family Policy Studies Centre, London.

Parker, J. (1975), Social Policy and Citizenship, Macmillan, London.

Parker, P. (1978), 'Reaching out to a wider network' Community Care, 18 October, pp.21-22.

Parker, R. (1981), 'Tending and social policy', Ch.2 of Goldberg, E.M. and Hatch, S. (eds.), 1981.

Pearlin, L.I. and Schooler, C. (1978), 'The structure of coping', Journal of Health and Social Behavior, Vol.19, pp.2-21.

Philip, M. and Duckworth, D. (1982), Children with Disabilities and their Families: a Review of Research, National Institute for Educational Research, London.

Pinker, R. (1971), Social Theory and Social Policy, Heinemann, London.

Pinker, R. (1974), 'Social policy and social justice', Journal of Social Policy, Vol.3, No.1, pp.1-19.

Pinker, R. (1979), The Idea of Welfare, Heinemann, London.

Poor Law Report (1974), The Poor Law Report of 1834, S.G. and E.O.A. Checkland (eds.), Penguin, Harmondsworth.

Reddin, M. (1977), Universality and Selectivity: Strategies in Social Policy, National Economic and Social Council, Stationery Office, Dublin.

Regional Trends, Great Britain (1984), (Volume 19), HMSO, London.

Rimmer, L. (1983), 'The economics of work and caring' in Finch, J. and Groves, D., 1983.

Roberts, H. (ed.) (1981), Women, Health and Reproduction, Routledge and Kegan Paul, London.

Robinson, A.S. (1984), The Plantation of Ulster, Gill and Macmillan, Dublin.

Robinson, F. and Abrams, P. (1977), What We Know about the Neighbours, Rowntree Research Unit, Durham.

Robinson, T. (1978), In Worlds Apart, Bedford Square Press, London.

Seebohm Report (1968), Report of the Committee on Local Authority and Allied Personal Social Services, Cmmd 3703, HMSO, London.

Selye, H. (1976), The Stress of Life, McGraw Hill, New York.

Seyd, R., Tennant, A. and Bayley, M. (1985), Old and Alone, (Neighbourhood Services Project - Dinnington, Paper No.10), Department of Sociological Studies, University of Sheffield, Sheffield.

Smith, G. (1986), 'Service delivery issues: towards a programme of research as a part of the future of welfare initiative' (a paper prepared for the initiative of the Social Affairs Committee of the ESRC on 'the future of welfare', presented at the School of Advanced Urban Studies, University of Bristol).

Spencer, H. (1851), Social Statics, Chapman, London.

Spencer, H. (1893), The Principles of Ethics, Vol.2, Williams and Norgate, London.

Stacey, M. (1975), Power, Persistence and Change: A Second Study of Banbury, Routledge and Kegan Paul, London.

Steiner, G.Y. (1966), Social Insecurity, Rand McNally, Chicago.

Timms, E. (1983), 'On the relevance of informal social networks to social work intervention', British Journal of Social Work, Vol.13, No.4, pp.405-415.

Titmuss, R.M. (1958), Essays on 'The Welfare State', Allen and Unwin, London.

Townsend, P. (1979), Poverty in the United Kingdom, Penguin, Harmondsworth.

Townsend, P. (1963), The Family Life of Old People, Penguin, Harmondsworth.

Tunstall, J. (1966), Old and Alone, Routledge and Kegan Paul, London.

Ungerson, C. (1983), 'Women and caring: skills, tasks, and taboos', in Gamarnikow (ed.), 1983.

Voysey, M. (1975), A Constant Burden, Routledge and Kegan Paul, London.

Walker, A. (ed.) (1982), Community Care: The Family, The State and Social Policy, Blackwell, Oxford.

Walker, A. and Qureshi, H. (1983), Elderly Persons Support Units: Evaluation Project, 1984-87, Department of Sociological Studies, University of Sheffield, Sheffield.

Walker, A. and Townsend, P. (eds.) (1981), Disability in Britain: a Manifesto of Rights, Martin Robertson, Oxford.

Warnock Report (1978), Report of the Committee of Enquiry into the Education ofHandicapped Children and Young People, (Cmnd.7212), HMSO, London.

Warren, D.I. (1981), Helping Networks, Notre Dame Press, Notre Dame, Indiana.

Wellman, B. (1981), 'Applying network analysis to the study of support', in Gottlieb (ed.), 1981.

Wenger, G.C. (1981), The Elderly in the Community: Family Contacts, Social Integration and Community Involvement, Working Paper 18, Social Services in Rural Areas Research Project, University College of North Wales, Bangor.

Wenger, G. C. (1984), The Supportive Network, Allen and Unwin, London.

West, P., Illsley, R. and Kelman, H. (1984), 'Public preferences for the care of dependency groups', Social Science and Medicine, Vol.18, No.4, pp.287-295.

Whittaker, J.K. (1986), 'Formal and informal helping in child welfare services', Child Welfare, Vol.65, No.1, pp.17-25.

Whitten, N.E. and Wolfe, A. (1973), 'Network analysis', Ch.16 of Honigmann, J. (1973), Handbook of Social and Cultural Anthropology, Rand McNally, Chicago.

Williams, R. (1983), 'Concepts of health', Sociology, Vol.17, No.2. pp.185-205.

Wills, T.A. (ed.) (1982), Basic Processes in Helping Relationships, Academic Press, London.

Wolfenden Report (1978), The Future of Voluntary Organisations, Croom Helm, London.

Young, M. and Willmott, P. (1962), Family and Kinship in East London, Penguin, Harmondsworth.

Young, M. and Willmott, P. (1973), The Symmetrical Family, Routledge and Kegan Paul, London.

Index

Abrams, P.	15, 52, 116
agriculture (see farms/farmers)	
altruism	7, 9, 15
Barclay Committee	1, 5-10, 114, 117
Bayley, M.	1, 104, 117
care, and caring and tending	57-69, and passim
Catholic(s)	14, 16, 19, 20, 22, 23, 25, 27, 32, 48, 49, 81, 97, 112
Church of Ireland	19, 33
clergy/priest/ minister(s)	18, 23-25, 59, 60, 72, 76, 111
clients	2, 6-11, 22, 99, 112, 113, 116, 117
community care	1, 14, 79, 116
doctor/G.P.	14, 18, 21, 24, 25, 58-60, 69, 74,76, 83, 112
education (see also school)	30, 78, 107, 115